W9-BHK-733

We're in This Together, Lord

Bible Devotions for Girls

Evelyn Amuedo Wade

Augsburg

MINNEAPOLIS

WE'RE IN THIS TOGETHER, LORD
Bible Devotions for Girls

Copyright © 1992 Augsburg Fortress. All rights reserved. Except for brief quotations in critical articles or reviews, no part of this book may be reproduced in any manner without prior written permission from the publisher. Write to: Permissions, Augsburg Fortress, 426 S. Fifth St., Box 1209, Minneapolis, MN 55440

Scripture quotations unless otherwise noted are from the Holy Bible, New International Version. Copyright © 1973, 1978, 1984 International Bible Society. Used by permission of Zondervan Bible Publishers.

The stories "Champions Stand Tall," "Just Martha," "Best Friends" (originally titled "But I'm Supposed To") and "It All Sounded So Logical" (originally titled "Satan's Mischief") first appeared in *Guide Magazine*.

Cover design: Eric Lecy
Photos: Superstock: cover, 52; Jim Whitmer: 32, 42, 62, 80; Robert Cushman Hayes: 20, 110, 120.

Library of Congress Cataloging-in-Publication Data

Wade, Evelyn Amuedo.
  We're in this together, Lord : Bible devotions for girls / Evelyn Amuedo Wade.
    p.   cm. — (Young readers)
  Summary: Twelve short stories address such issues as cheating, secret organizations, shoplifting, and treatment of the elderly and handicapped. Each story is followed by questions for discussion.
  ISBN 0-8066-2649-6 :
  1. Girls—Prayer-books and devotions—English.   2. Short stories, American.   [1. Conduct of life.   2. Christian life.   3. Prayer books and devotions.]   I. Title.   II. Series.
BV4860.W33   1992
242'.62—dc20   92-30987
                                                              CIP
                                                               AC

The paper used in this publication meets the minimum requirements of American National Standards for Information Sciences–Permanence of Paper for Printed Library Materials, ANSI Z329.48-1984. ∞™

Manufactured in the U.S.A.   AF 9-2649

96   95   94   93   92   1   2   3   4   5   6   7   8   9   10

The Crossroads Library
Mt. Olive Lutheran Church
3045 Chicago Ave.
Minneapolis, MN 55407

We're in This Together, Lord

*In Memory of Jim,
my husband and my closest friend*

Contents

A Note to the Reader

Meet the girls from the town of Japonica—Babe, Wendy, Martha, Penny, Hilary, Nora, Jennifer, Jill, Tracy, Bonita, Alexis, and Cecily. They all go to the same school, swim at the same pool, and attend the same summer camp. They are all good friends. And they are all young Christians growing up in a sometimes confusing world, just like you are.

The stories in this book deal with some of the real issues that face kids today. As you read them, you will see that every now and then even the nicest kids in the neighborhood can be tempted to do things that they know in their hearts are wrong. We hope that these stories and the Scripture on which they are based will help you when you have to make hard decisions.

Before each story there is a Bible passage. Read it carefully and commit it to your heart. The characters in these stories have learned to rely on the words of Scripture. You, too, can draw strength from God's Word. Following each story there is a prayer and some questions to ask yourself. Take the time to read these and consider how you might have acted if you had been the character in the story.

We hope that you will enjoy meeting the kids from Japonica and that their adventures can help you in your own. May God be with you on your journey!

Champions Stand Tall

"Watch and pray so that you will not fall into temptation. The spirit is willing, but the body is weak."   Mark 14:38

◆   ◆   ◆

Babe Remberton was about to win the biggest award of her life. Then the circumstances changed. . . .

◆   ◆   ◆

Three sharp whistle blasts from Charlotte, our swim coach. We all knew what that signal meant. Time for swim practice. No more free swimming.

"All out!" Her voice snapped through the air like the whip of a lion tamer, and everyone hushed. Pride in our team ran deep.

In no time the pool emptied, and all of us huddled together around the decks. A shiver of excitement trembled through my veins. This was my magic year—twelve years old and I was about to win the biggest award of my life—the blue ribbon for first place in my class. I could feel it in my bones. It was the thing I wanted most in life.

"You'll walk away with it, Babe," Charlotte had told me. "You're a champ!"

Babe. That's what everyone called me. I am nowhere near the athlete that Babe Ruth was. But I got the nickname when I was about nine, the day I hit a home run playing Little League baseball. It was really a lucky hit because I'm not a good player. But the ball sailed into the air as if it was headed for the moon.

Dr. Weaver, a good friend of my father's, nudged Dad. "Wow! Look at that ball go!" he screamed, watching it arc through the sky. "Mark, you've got another Babe Ruth on your hands! She's a real champ!"

And I've been called "Babe" or "The Champ" ever since.

It's swimming, though, that's my real love. From the time I was two years old, my mother used to take me down to the little wading pool every day. We have long, sizzling summers in Japonica. Now at twelve, I'd become a good swimmer—one of the best on our team.

Today we were practicing for the upcoming tournament where I'd really show my stuff.

"Okay, kids," Charlotte began. "We'll take the fifty-inch girls first. Line up for measuring."

In our county tournaments, height determines what class a kid swims in.

Every week Charlotte measured us faithfully. "You kids grow too fast," she explained. "I don't want you practicing for one class only to find you've outgrown it the day of the tournament." Last year I was swimming in the sixty-inch class, and when the pool opened this summer, I'd already grown into the next tallest group.

We all began talking and joking around as we lined up.

Then two quick whistle blasts. This meant silence. The racket stopped.

"Now here's the word," Charlotte said. "One peep out of anyone and you're out. O-U-T out!" She raised her hand and crooked her thumb toward the gate. "We're here for two things only. To swim—and who knows what else?"

A hundred voices screamed out together, "To win!"

Charlotte grinned. "Right! To win!" She held her clasped hands above her head as a sign of victory.

If you think Charlotte's tough, you're right. She was boss, and she tolerated no nonsense. For the last four years, ever since she was eighteen, she'd been a lifeguard at our pool and responsible for coaching the team.

In the process, she'd built up a team we could be proud of. I adored her. She'd really worked with me, helping me perfect my stroke, teaching me how to dive, timing me, and best of all giving me the kind of encouragement I needed.

She'd even mentioned the Olympics on occasion. "You've got the body for it, Champ," she said to me once, punching me playfully on the arm. "Even better, you've got the winning spirit." I was not alone. She worked with everyone she thought had a chance to become a winner.

Now Charlotte took us to one of the dressing rooms and carefully measured us, one after the other, against the long measuring rule tacked onto the wall. Finally it was my turn.

That was when disaster struck. I could see the frown on her face even before she told me. Already I'd gone over the five-foot-six-inch limit. I'd have to swim in the "Unlimited" Class. I slumped away from the rule as if I'd been beaten.

"Five feet, six-and-a-half inches." She said it several times with a look as gloomy as the underside of the old bayou bridge. Then "Get back up here, Babe. Let me measure you again."

"Scrunch down, Babe!" Cecily Adams yelled. "Hunch your shoulders."

But no one listened. We were all too thunderstruck. There was no way I could win or even place in the Unlimited class. They swam two full laps for the race. I was only twelve, and I'd have to swim against girls sixteen and seventeen years old. They'd make me look like a turtle and not the one who took the race from the famous hare.

"What'll we do?" Tracy Andrews moaned. "Babe's got to win a blue if we're going to win the banner at the end."

"We'll do it," Charlotte said. "Babe'll win her blue, and we will win the banner." Having just graduated from college and with a full-time teaching job waiting for her in the fall, this would be Charlotte's last year at the pool. We'd never won the banner yet, and with our pool hosting this year's tournament I knew how much it meant to her.

I felt like a traitor. According to the point system used at the tournament, I had to take a first in my class for us to win the banner. We'd swum against those other pools often enough to know what to expect in each contest.

For the next few weeks, I worked with true dedication. I swam daily, raced with Cecily Adams and Tracy Andrews and a couple of others in Unlimited. I ate, drank, and slept exactly as Charlotte told me to, but I knew I wasn't making it.

I remember one day what a discouraged little group we were walking home from the pool. When I left some of my friends at the corner, I felt dejected and a little angry at myself. Then Cecily and Tracy caught up with me.

"Come on, now. Don't look so unhappy," Cecily said.

"It's not that bad," Tracy echoed.

But by the expressions on their faces and the breathy way they spoke, I could tell they had more on their minds than team spirit.

"OK, what's up?" I said.

Tracy smiled. "Nothing's—"

"Look, Babe," Cecily interrupted. "We'll get to the point fast. You can win that race if you want to, but you've got to do exactly as we say. OK?"

A cold shiver ran up my back. I didn't know what it was all about, but whatever it was, I didn't like it.

"You've seen Sadie Meeks run interference for Hamilton, haven't you?" Cecily asked.

"Sure I have, but it isn't fair."

"No, it isn't. But she wins races for her pool."

"We'll run interference for you, Babe," Tracy said bluntly. "We'll sacrifice for you this year, and you can sacrifice for one of us next year. Here's the plan."

I barely listened. I knew the plan. We'd all dive in, but "somehow" Cecily would get tangled up in the water with one of my opponents, Tracy would mess up another, and I'd come sailing in first.

In big cities they have big Olympic-sized pools and barriers to keep this from happening. We don't have that kind of money in Japonica, and our pools are much smaller.

"But that's cheating," I protested.

"It's not cheating at all," Tracy answered flatly. "It's technique. It's strategy. Besides, if they do it to us, don't they deserve to have us do it to them?"

"Yeah, I guess they do," I said uncertainly. Maybe they were right. I was still burning from that race the year before when somebody from the Hillsboro pool ran interference on me, and I took a red ribbon when I really should have had a blue.

"And don't tell Charlotte," Cecily warned when they left me at my front gate. "She'd be furious."

I walked into the house slowly, deep in thought. My joy in the meet vanished. My mind was confused.

Mom sensed it almost immediately. "What's the matter, honey? Something go wrong at the pool?"

"I guess I'm kind of tired," I answered. "I'll feel better after supper."

I didn't feel better. I felt worse. But somehow by the next morning, I wasn't quite so worried. I was beginning to see the justice of the plan. We'd taken a beating too often by those other kids. We'd just be paying them back.

That day at the pool, Cecily practiced side-swiping Tracy, but since we were all on the same team, Charlotte didn't notice. Every day my speed increased, and she'd get so excited clocking me, that's all she could think about.

"See how easy that was?" Cecily asked on the way home. "We've got it all worked out. In three days you'll be the big winner. The pride of Japonica!"

I spent the rest of the day really worried. I had to win, and I knew now that I could. But if winning made me feel like this, I wasn't so sure I wanted to win. I tried praying. Sometimes when I pray, the Lord gives me an idea of what I should do, but even prayer didn't seem to work.

I walked around like a spook for two days, arguing with myself. *Why shouldn't I pay back those cheats for what they did to me last year? But it's wrong*, I answered back. *Sure, but. . . .*

Friday afternoon, the day before the big competition, I made up my mind. I'd speak to Pastor Blanchard. He had a wonderful way of listening, and I knew he'd understand. So after practice, I detoured when I left the others and headed toward his house. He was home. His car was in the driveway.

17

But suddenly, as I stood there at the gate, I could imagine his face—just the way he'd look at me as I told my story. He'd just sit there looking me right in the eye, sort of smiling, but listening to every word. And when I finished talking, he'd say, real gentle, "Rosemary, (That's my real name.) what do you think?"

I knew the answer. I knew I could never cheat. What joy would I have in a blue ribbon, anyway, if I hadn't won it honestly? My prayers had been answered after all. I didn't need to disturb Pastor Blanchard.

I turned around and started walking home.

The following day I found Cecily and Tracy and set them straight. There'd be no interference in my race. In a way, I think they looked a little relieved. I guess they had felt guilty, too.

Well, I guess you know the outcome. I didn't come in first. In fact I didn't win a ribbon at all. I came floundering in fourth amid all the screaming and yelling for the big winners. But you know what? My gang from Japonica was still rooting for me even after the race was over. And I knew I had won an even more important match.

For many years, my friends had called me "The Champ." I'd finally learned to act like one.

LET'S TALK ABOUT IT

1. Considering that Babe had been cheated out of the ribbon she deserved, wouldn't she have been justified in going along with Cecily and Tracy's plan?

2. If you were in some kind of competition, would winning be the most important thing to consider?

3. Do you think the kids in Japonica were lucky or not to have a leader like Charlotte?

4. Have you ever had a problem that you didn't want to discuss with your parents? Why do you think this is?

5. Since Cecily and Tracy weren't going to benefit personally by the arrangement they suggested, do you think they would have been guilty of cheating?

6. How did you feel when Babe decided to swim her own race without help? Were you pleased with her decision? Were you disappointed with the outcome of the race? Do you think she was foolish not to take advantage of such a generous offer from her friends?

◆　◆　◆

Please, Lord, give me the courage to lose if necessary, rather than to cheat. It's nice to win, but not like that. Even if no one ever knew it but me, the award would mean nothing if I had to cheat to get it.

A Boyfriend All Her Own

"For we are God's workmanship, created in Christ Jesus to do good works, which God prepared in advance for us to do."   Ephesians 2:10

◆　◆　◆

When the Powells and their thirteen-year-old son came to visit Wendy Weaver's mother, Wendy couldn't have been more excited, until. . . .

◆　◆　◆

"Hey! Great! Wonderful!"

That was my mom. Real off the wall, you know? The mail had just come in, and she was reading a letter, throwing in those little one-word comments. I could actually hear the exclamation points!

At least it was *good* news. If it had been bad news, she could have been saying, "How awful! How dreadful!"

I was dying to hear what it was all about, but you don't interrupt my mom when she's in one of her raptures. So I just clammed up and let her finish the letter.

Finally she put it down, and the glow in her eyes could have lit up Mammoth Cave. "What do you think? You've heard me speak about my friend Connie Powell?"

I grinned. "How could I miss? She was your roomie in college. She was the one elected cutest girl on your floor. She was the one who introduced you to Dad." I was ticking them off on my fingers. "She was the one who gave you the home perm, and your hair fell out. She was the one—"

"Don't be smart, Wendy." Mom gave me her famous that-will-be-enough-out-of-you look. But she was too happy about her friend coming to be really steamed.

"I'm sorry, Mom."

"I haven't seen Connie since graduation." Mom was off again—kind of dreamy.

"And?"

"Oh." Mom came back to life. "And now she's coming here to spend the summer." Her face glowed with joy.

"The whole summer? Here?" My heart wobbled like someone on a high wire who's just missed a step. I could just see myself playing gopher for the duration.

"Not in our house, Wendy," Mom said, dismissing my concern as if she were getting rid of a man at the door selling cemetery plots. "She wants me to find her an apartment. Her husband's a social scientist, and they're coming south on some kind of research he's conducting in this part of the state."

"That's super." I tried for enthusiasm, but to tell the truth, I couldn't have cared less.

Mom was still raving. "I'm so excited! Let me read you the part about her son."

I began to perk up.

"I'll be needing at least two bedrooms, as I'm bringing Jeff along too. He goes to camp as a rule during July and August, but now that he's in eighth grade he's going away to school in the fall, and I want him with me for the summer."

Wow! Jeff! "You didn't tell me she had a son."

"Didn't I? I'm sorry, honey. I guess I didn't think you'd be interested. And she so rarely mentioned him in her cards."

Isn't that just like a mother? The most important thing about her friend, and my mom forgets. To me it sounded like having a built-in boyfriend for the summer. I'd get invited to everything! Can you imagine anyone giving a party and not inviting the new guy in town? And, of course, the girl he was visiting. Me—Wendy Weaver—twelve years old, and I get a boyfriend practically thrown at me. I couldn't wait to tell Martha Hicks, my best friend.

Mom looked kind of anxious. "You won't mind introducing him around, will you, Wendy?" she asked.

"Mind? Why should I mind?" I minded as much as a prisoner minds being released from jail.

"You usually don't like boys."

"For gosh sakes, Mom, I got over that when I was ten."

"Great! You'll be having your birthday in a few weeks. Maybe you can have a party. Would you like that?"

"Sure! I'd love it! Can I tell Martha?"

"If you want to. Just think, eighteen years since we've seen each other."

Mom was off in the stratosphere again when she left to answer the letter. And I was kind of spaced out myself. I called Martha, and we talked for an hour about the fun we'd be having this summer.

By the time my mom's friend was due the following week, Mom and I had everything ready. I helped find a furnished apartment, I'd told everybody about Jeff, and I'd already begun inviting people to the party.

But mostly I just daydreamed of Jeff going to the pool with me, joining in our picnics, and meeting us at church. I could just see him—tall, good-looking, fun. By now I even had him in a snazzy uniform. Since his mom said he'd be going away to school, I assumed it would be a military academy.

But then I began to worry.

"Suppose he doesn't like me," I said to Martha the day before they came.

"He will. After all, his mom is your mom's best friend."

"I know. But I'm not exactly the prettiest girl in Japonica."

"Close to it. And you're sure the nicest."

You see why Martha's my best friend? Even so, I was still nervous. It would be just my luck that he would fall for someone else, and there would go my first real boyfriend.

I was also kind of antsy about the music for the party. Everyone played music at parties, and I didn't have many tapes.

"People will lend theirs," Martha assured me. "Don't worry."

But I did worry. At the last party at Hilary Lawson's house, everyone's tapes and CD's got mixed up, and a lot of people said they'd never lend theirs out again.

Mom and I cleaned the house until it shone, and Cullen mowed the lawn and weeded the garden. Cullen's my brother. A year older than I am and already rounding up guys for the party.

I had everything planned and had invited ten other girls besides Martha. Mom stocked the refrigerator with food. We were all set for the biggest event of my whole, entire life.

The afternoon they were to arrive, I made a pitcher of lemonade, and Mom had a casserole ready to pop into the oven for supper that night.

"You and Cullen and Jeff can take turns at the ice cream freezer," she said.

I kept running to look out of the big front window to see if they'd arrived yet. Finally a station wagon pulled up, and I could see this blond kid in the back seat. I knew it had to be Jeff.

At first my excitement could have set off a carload of fireworks, but I noticed he seemed awkward as he tumbled out of the car. And then I noticed that he was kind of fat. I hate fat guys.

My excitement level plunged to zero on the Richter scale, but then I thought, *What difference does it make, as long as he's nice.* He had to be nice. My whole life depended on it.

Mr. and Ms. Powell got out of the wagon and headed for our house. Jeff followed. The nearer they got, the more I knew that something was wrong. It was the way he walked—little bitty steps—and he shuffled his feet and looked at the ground. He was close enough now for me to tell. He was retarded!

I knew that look. I'd seen enough retarded kids on the playground of the special school near my grandmother's house in Virginia.

I glanced at Mom. She looked shocked too. "Mom!" It was both an accusation and a cry for help.

But my mom's a true Christian. She got control of herself immediately. "Honey, God makes people the way God sees fit. Our Creator loves us all the same," she said. "I'm sure Jeff is a lovely boy. And I know your friends will like him."

I wasn't so sure. She didn't know my friends the way I did. And I'd been doing all this bragging. For three weeks my friends had heard nothing out of me but Jeff this and Jeff that. Now I had to go back and tell everyone he was handicapped. That's the way Mom said I should describe him instead of retarded.

There was no time to say any more. Mom rushed out with her arms wide open, and she and Ms. Powell grabbed each other in a big hug. Then Dad followed,

26

and Cullen joined them. Everybody was introducing everybody else, and Mom even hugged Jeff. I thought I'd die. I sure hoped no one expected *me* to hug anyone.

With their arms around each other's waist, Mom and Ms. Powell headed for the house and the rest of us followed.

When Ms. Powell introduced Jeff to me, I tried to be friendly, but I must say that Cullen did a better job than I did. And Jeff wouldn't even look at us.

I called Martha as soon as I could.

"Oh, Wendy, that's awful! But, look, it's not your fault."

"I know, but I'm so embarrassed."

"Why should you be embarrassed? He's probably an OK guy when you get to know him. Do you want me to come over?"

"No. Not now. Maybe tonight."

I hung up and went back to the living room where Cullen was working hard, trying to be friendly. Mom and Ms. Powell worked in the kitchen putting supper on while Dad and Mr. Powell went back outside and wandered around among the flower beds.

Cullen looked up as I entered the room. "I was just telling Jeff about our party," he said.

Jeff kept looking down at the floor. "I don't like parties," he replied in a flat, toneless voice. It was as if he'd never heard a note of music in his life, and here I'd been thinking of drafting him for the choir.

My impulse was to excuse myself—to help in the kitchen, anything to get out of talking to Jeff. But I couldn't do that to my brother.

"At least we could sit down," I said. Jeff sat gingerly on the edge of a straight chair as if he was afraid someone might snatch it out from under him. Cullen and I sat on the couch.

"I bet you'd like *this* party," Cullen said, working hard. "My sister has invited some of the prettiest girls in town."

Jeff hunched his shoulders and avoided our eyes. He was moving his legs back and forth, hitting his knees together in a kind of rhythm.

"How about chess?" Cullen asked. "Want to play some chess?"

Jeff shook his head. "I don't like games."

"Music?" Poor Cullen was really trying.

Suddenly Jeff looked up. He still didn't look directly at us, but now he was alive.

His mother stood at the doorway, smiling. "Oh, you've hit it all right. If there's one thing Jeff does love, it's music." She turned to Jeff. "We'll unpack some of your tapes, honey. Ask Daddy to do it."

"He has tapes?" I asked. "Popular tapes?" I hated myself because I knew all I was thinking about was me. Me and my party. Why couldn't I have cared about him the way Cullen was doing?

Ms. Powell laughed again. "He has everything."

While Jeff was gone, I heard his mother talking to Mom. Seriously. Telling Mom what was wrong with him.

Apparently, he was very sick with some kind of terrible high fever when he was in the first grade. When he recovered, his mind never developed beyond six years old except for this interest in music.

"He may never be able to earn a living," his mother was saying. "That's why we're sending him away to school. They have new techniques that may help him."

When Jeff returned with his tape deck and a couple of boxes of tapes, he was like a different person—alive, sure of himself, on his own ground. I found him interesting.

At first I was afraid he'd turn out to be one of those long-hair musicians who understood music theory and all that kind of boring stuff. But that wasn't his specialty at all. He knew a fantastic amount of information about the music as a product. He could take any piece and tell you who wrote it, in what year, who did the video, who were the back-up singers, how many tapes had been sold, how much money it made, and—oh, everything you could imagine. And I mean old stuff and everything. It was truly amazing, especially considering how unmusical his voice sounded.

His mother called him an *idiot savant*, which sounded, at first, like an insult. But that's what someone with his sickness is called.

Once, when Jeff answered some far-out question Cullen had asked him, I turned to Ms. Powell and asked, "Wouldn't it be great to have a guy like Jeff working in the library? So you don't have to go searching through half a dozen research books."

"Yes, a music librarian," his mom replied. "What a great idea, Wendy!"

Jeff still avoided our eyes, and he still spoke in that flat monotone, but he was more relaxed now, and I realized he'd been terribly frightened before. If I was nervous meeting him, imagine how nervous he must have been meeting all of us.

Later, Martha came over. It was like a game, asking Jeff about music, trying to stump him. And you know something else? I was proud of him—like he was my special find!

I know this much. His parents were sure proud of him. I never knew that handicapped people could be so much fun or that their parents really care about them the way Mr. and Ms. Powell obviously did. The three of them had their little jokes just like any family. Although Jeff never did smile or drop the little mannerisms he had in the beginning, somehow it didn't matter.

He was who he was, the way God had made him. And God loved him just as God loved everyone else. In my own way, I guess I loved Jeff too.

LET'S TALK ABOUT IT

1. Have you ever known a handicapped person well?
2. How do you think you would feel if some accident left you with a severe handicap?
3. Occasionally you hear people ridicule a person with a handicap. Why do you think this is?
4. Do you think Wendy or Martha acted in a more Christian way?
5. What about Cullen? Why was he more able to accept Jeff's condition than Wendy? Would the same thinking apply to Martha?
6. Do you think you could learn to feel love for someone like Jeff the way that Wendy did?

◆ ◆ ◆

Dear God, help me to see the goodness and the beauty in everyone, regardless of how smart they may or may not be. Who am I to judge others, anyway? And thank you, Lord, for making me the way I am.

Just Martha

"There are different kinds of gifts, but the same Spirit. There are different kinds of service, but the same Lord. There are different kinds of working, but the same God works all of them in all men."

1 Corinthians 12:4-6

♦   ♦   ♦

Martha Hicks was convinced she was totally worthless. But does God ever make anyone completely without worth?

♦   ♦   ♦

Twelve years old. The third girl in a family of three. That's me. Martha Hicks. The only one with no talent, no beauty, no nothing. Oh, yes, I can dust and clean well.

"Martha's a whiz around the house," Mom bragged to a friend of hers. "She goes at the kitchen with both hands flying. And before I have a chance to think about it, she has everything as neat as a pin."

And you know what? She meant it as a compliment! Big deal.

My mom the fashion artist. Married to Dad the architect. Both of them parents of Sarah the artist, Rachel the pianist, and Martha the blob. So there you have us—our very own cast for "The Young and the Restless." Young and ambitious, restless to grow up and be famous. Talent, talent, talent—plus Mitey Mouse, the little housewife.

Mom and Dad have always read their Bibles before they go to bed at night, and all our names came right out of Scripture. The night before I was born they'd been reading about Martha, sister of Lazarus. Ergo— my name.

The perfect name for me because I'm the perfect Martha—duty-first, drab little Martha.

Before I came along, though, with my little mop and my dust pan, they had those two talented little darlings—Sarah, who's been able to draw and paint from the time she was six years old, and Rachel, who plays the piano as if the music rolled right out of those long, pretty fingers.

Imagine me playing the piano—me with my sawed-off hands and stubby fingers!

What I really hate to imagine is the day I was born. The third kid. The third girl! This is the way it probably happened.

"Oh, no!" That's Dad that you hear. Groaning. "Not another girl!"

And Mom sympathizing. "I'm sorry, Bart. I know you wanted a boy."

I can just see him. He puts his finger in my hand, and my stubby fingers grasp it. "Hey! Look at that hold." He smiles. "A husky little thing. She'll be a big help around the house. Yes, we'll definitely have to name her Martha."

I wonder how he could tell. But he was right. I'm the Wonder of the Washer. The Queen of the Kitchen. The Guru of the Garden. If you want your weeds pulled, your lawn mowed, your house cleaned, just ask Martha the blob.

So when Wendy called and asked me to sign up for one of the Youth Programs our church was organizing, naturally I said, "N-o-o-o-o way!"

Wendy's my best friend, and in a way she's like Sarah and Rachel—creative.

"Come on, Martha," she urged. "We'll have fun."

"*You'll* have fun," I corrected. "But there's nothing I can do. I'd just be in the way."

"No you won't. Anyway, Pastor Blanchard asked specifically that I get you involved."

"Why me? I don't have a creative bone in my whole body."

Pastor Blanchard had been talking about these new projects for weeks. Several grown-ups in the church had volunteered to sponsor various groups. They had no trouble getting volunteers. The adults of our church are always gung ho for anything that keeps their kids out of trouble.

The problem was all the groups were doing creative kinds of things. There was the music group, the art group, the writing group, the photography group. They even had a flower-arranging group. And if there's one thing I'm not, it's creative. I'm all thumbs on two left hands when it comes to any kind of creativity.

"The one I'd like to work on," Wendy said, "is the youth paper. If you signed up with me, you wouldn't have to do anything."

"Fun!" I grunted. "Sitting around, getting in everyone's way."

But I went with her because I'm the typical patsy that anyone can push around.

All of this is to explain how I eventually ended up on the staff of *The Wordsmiths*. That's what we decided to call the paper that by now is a going concern, reporting on what the other groups are doing.

The others on the staff are Jennifer Renquist, Alexis Colenko, Ted Copeland, and Bryan Remberton. Six of us altogether, counting Wendy and me, with Susan Wilburn as sponsor. Susan isn't exactly an adult. She's still in college, but she's majoring in journalism and was dying to handle this particular youth group.

I'll never forget the first day we got together. We were to meet in the storeroom because an old sink in that room blocked off a bleak little area we could use as a darkroom for developing film. (That *they* could use, would be more accurate.) But the sight of that room was enough to discourage anyone. Some of the kids almost backed out. Even Susan looked a little green around the gills.

Crates of old dishes stood in the doorway, a big basket of beat-up pots and pans leaned against a rickety table, and boxes of tarnished knives and forks jumbled together on the top of the table. Cartons of old menus leaned perilously against an old gas water heater, and a shaky-looking file cabinet stood out like a sad specter with half the drawers hanging open.

We'd recently bought the building from some restaurant owner to make it into an annex for the church. But I don't suppose anyone had thought about how ratty the storeroom was.

The floor was grubby, the table and two rickety straight chairs were thick with dust, and the faded old curtains at the windows hung against grimy window panes.

Curiously, as depressed as this place made the others feel, I saw it as an interesting challenge. "It's not so bad," I said. "We can clean it up in no time if everyone will chip in and work."

Mentally, I began to divide the room into workable areas, figuring out what had to be done first to simplify what would have to come next.

I looked over the group. Any minute there would be a general strike. Alexis was inspecting her finger nails. Jennifer glanced at the door.

"What about next week?" Ted asked. "Why don't we start then?"

"Right," Wendy agreed. "How can we clean up when we have nothing to clean with? Next week we can bring pails and mops and stuff."

I surveyed the junk on the floor. Those big soup kettles could double as pails, I decided. We could tear up the curtains for scrub cloths.

Recovering from her initial shock, Susan said, "Of course, we'll work. What do you want us to do?"

"OK," I said, suddenly taking charge. "The first thing is to get rid of the clutter. Ted, you and Bryan start loading those boxes into my dad's car. I'll ask him to drop them off at Good Will some time. Susan, if you'll rip those curtains off the windows, you and the girls can start tearing them into good-sized pieces for rags."

There were a few groans from the girls, but, miraculously, they went to work.

While the others were busy with the jobs I'd given them, I inspected the water heater. I decided that all it needed was to be turned on. At least I could try.

Finding a packet of matches in a drawer under the sink, I lighted it, and, *voila!* It worked. Then I checked out the rest of the kitchen to see what else I could find. Sure enough, in one of the cupboards there was a dried up bar of soap and a leftover bottle of vinegar, more than half full.

"Anyone have a pen knife?" I asked, and each of the boys came up with one.

There's no point in giving you a blow-by-blow description of what we did to clean up that room. But clean it up we did. All of us were working on our hands and knees before it was over. The soap chipped into hot water made wonderful suds, and the vinegar was the best grease cutter you could imagine.

That revolting sink turned out to be gleaming white porcelain with good fixtures once I polished them. And from under all that dirt the floor emerged as a soft, pleasant green linoleum.

When we finally stopped to rest, we were tired and stiff. And, yes, our hands were a mess. But somehow we felt triumphant.

"Martha, you're a genius," Susan said.

I laughed. "Me? A genius? All I'm good for is housework. I'm just Martha, remember?"

"That's very true," Susan replied, "but believe me, it's the Marthas of the world who keep the rest of us going. You're a genius at organization. That's why you're such a good housekeeper. You know just where to start. And you know how to organize your energy and time. You attacked this job with both hands flying."

I suddenly remembered that those were the very words my mom had used when she'd bragged about me to her friend.

"My aunt has a terrific job as an executive in one of the biggest hotels in Chicago," Susan said. "And you know what her job is? She's the housekeeper. She has hundreds of employees under her supervision. They are the ones who make the beds and keep the entire hotel clean. You could have a career like that too, Martha."

"I never thought of that," I told her.

"I think God has given you talent for cleaning," Susan continued, "and you're using it well. You're serving God by doing housework just as creatively as the person who designs a worship banner or leads the choir. Just look at which you've accomplished here today."

We all looked around. The room sparkled. OK, so it was still kind of shabby, but it *was* clean.

The next week Susan brought in some old curtains she had at home, and we plan to give the walls a coat of paint some day soon. My dad exchanged all those old dishes and things for a manual typewriter and a dictionary at Good Will, and we're getting out *The Wordsmiths* regularly each week.

Our group voted for Wendy to be the editor. The others are all reporters. And what do you think they voted me to be? I'm the managing editor, of all things. Me, the blob who thought she had no talent.

LET'S TALK ABOUT IT

1. Why do you think Martha was so sure she had no talent?
2. Do you agree with Susan that housekeeping can be just as creative and important, in its own way, as singing, painting, or playing the piano?
3. Besides supervising the original cleanup job, how do you think Martha showed her true value in working with *The Wordsmiths?*
4. Do you think God has a scale on which we are rated, or does God truly love us all the same?
5. How did both Martha and Wendy show their talent for friendship? Do you think friendship is a talent?
6. What are some of your own talents?

♦ ♦ ♦

Dear God, when my spirits are low, I often feel worthless too. Help me, Lord, to appreciate the talents you have given me and to use them fully. Also, help me to understand that you don't make any worthless things or people.

Penny-Wise

"Keep me from deceitful ways; be gracious to me through your law."   Psalm 119:29

◆   ◆   ◆

Penny Renquist's greatest desire was to own a dog. Her dream was about to come true when complications arose. Penny had to change her whole approach.

◆   ◆   ◆

"Hey, Penny! Wait for me!"

From a block away, I could hear Hilary Lawson's voice. Hilary is in my class at school and we go to the same church.

She was breathing hard when she caught up with me at the corner.

"Did you hear about the Bellamys?" She panted. "They're moving to Florida."

"Florida! Why?"

"That's where their son lives. Anyway, my mother said it's because of Mr. Bellamy's health. The winters here are hard on old people, and they want a warmer climate."

I hardly knew the Bellamys, but I did know Flower, their beautiful collie. I couldn't stand to think of losing her. Someone said Mrs. Bellamy named her dog Flower because she's a "collie" flower. I wouldn't have thought Mrs. Bellamy had that much of a sense of humor. From a distance she looked so cross. But you never know.

For the past two years, every time I passed their side yard, I'd stop to pet Flower through the chain-link fence. She waited for me by the garage. Sometimes I could see her ears pricked, listening for the sound of my footsteps even before I got there.

Then when she'd see me, she'd go wild with excitement, kind of whining and crying until I rounded the corner, then practically leaping the fence to get to me.

"When are they moving?" I asked.

"In a couple of weeks," Hilary answered. "Mom said they bought a condominium in Tampa and are already packing. Now—here's where you come in. They can't have a pet in the condo, so Mrs. Bellamy's hunting for someone to give Flower to."

My heart skipped a beat. "To give Flower to! Do you think?" Already my mind was moving that collie into my yard.

"I sure do. Seems to me you're the obvious choice. That's why I was in such a hurry to catch up with you."

My mind whirled. I didn't even know Mrs. Bellamy. Why would she give that beautiful dog to a twelve-year-old girl she knew nothing about? Yet why not? No one could love that dog more.

From the fringes of my argument with myself, I could hear Hilary still talking.

". . . so when Mom told me about it, I thought, *Penny Renquist is just the one.*"

"But I don't even know Mrs. Bellamy."

"Jennifer does."

I stopped in my tracks. Yes! Jennifer worked for her last year. Jennifer is my twin sister. She minded Flower when the Bellamys went to Florida to visit their son at Christmas. Which was crazy because Jennifer doesn't even like animals. Anyway, if my sister could put in a good word for me. . . .

"Don't you pass by the Bellamys' house on your way home?" Hilary asked.

"Sure."

"Then why don't you stop in and ask her? It can't hurt."

"You don't think I should ask Jenny first?"

"No. Get in your bid before someone else comes along."

All my life I've wanted a dog, but we lived for so long in an apartment building on Washington Avenue that having a pet of any kind was impossible. Mom always promised that if we ever moved into a house with a yard, I could have one.

Then last month we did exactly that. We bought the old Crichton place with this huge backyard, and I was only waiting for my family to simmer down after the move before I started talking about a dog again. Now the whole thing was like a complicated puzzle with most of the pieces beginning to fit into place.

After Hilary turned off to go to her house, I walked on slowly, my mind racing with a dozen thoughts.

I stood for a minute outside Mrs. Bellamy's house. Then I took a deep breath, marched up the steps, and rang the bell.

Mrs. Bellamy answered almost immediately. For an elderly lady she stood very straight and looked much taller than she seemed from a distance. Her skin fitted neatly over the bones of her face, and her eyes matched the cold gray color of her hair.

I was so nervous I couldn't speak.

Finally she said, "Yes?"

"I'm . . . I'm . . ."

"I know who you are. You're the Renquist girl. What can I do for you?"

I kept thinking, *If only she'd smile or something.* But she didn't.

I took a deep breath. "It's about Flower. I heard you were hunting for someone to take care of her, and I—"

She looked at me sternly. "And you thought you'd offer yourself for the job."

"Well, yes ma'am," I said. Then it all came tumbling out at once. "I really love Flower, Mrs. Bellamy. And I'd take extra-good care of her. I'd feed her and comb her and bathe her and—well, whatever is necessary to handle her right."

Her eyes narrowed as she gave me a strange look. Although she didn't really smile, there was a hint of a smile in her eyes. I knew I'd made an impression. Beginning to feel a tiny bit confident, I let myself relax.

"Yes," she said, "I suppose you'd do OK. You certainly did a good job when you minded her last year."

I nearly flipped! She thought I was Jennifer.

I murmured, "Yes ma'am," and looked away.

"Well," she said. "Let me think about it. Do you have your parents' permission to have a dog?"

"Yes ma'am. Er, no ma'am. Well, not really. But I know my mom will say yes." I was babbling at this point. Suddenly I wanted to get away as fast as I could.

"Well, you speak to your mother, and if she says it's OK, we'll talk about it again. This is no small responsibility, you understand. I want someone I can trust completely."

Somehow I got away. My head was spinning. All I had to do was let her go on thinking I was Jenny, and Flower was mine. But the last thing she said was that she wanted someone she could trust. Could she trust someone who pretended to be somebody else?

It was all so crazy. I'd do a better job than Jenny because I truly loved Flower. She had taken the job just to earn the money. Life seemed so unfair. I remember how disappointed I was at the time that Jennifer had been singled out like that when I should have gotten that job. In fact, I'd have done it for nothing.

All the way home my mind flopped from one way of thinking to another. What difference did it make who Mrs. Bellamy thought I was? What mattered was that Flower have a good home. No one could give that to her better than I could. On the other hand, if I started off with a big lie, could I really be trusted to take my responsibilities seriously?

Still, I'd feel like a fool if I told the truth and Mrs. Bellamy gave Flower to someone else. Who knows how well that person would take care of her? So, in the long run, it would really be worse for Flower that way. And wasn't it her happiness we were all thinking about?

By the time I got home, I was so exhausted from arguing with myself, putting up phony arguments, trying to arrive at a decision I could live with, that I didn't mention the dog to Mom. I knew if I talked to her alone, I wouldn't be able to look her in the eye, and she'd know right away that something was wrong.

Finally at dinner I brought it up. With Daddy, Jenny, and my two little brothers there, I hoped there'd be enough confusion for me to hide behind. Then when I did mention it, everyone was so excited—especially Billy and Tommy—that everything went as smooth as buttermilk. I got my parents' OK and

Jennifer thought it was great. All I needed now was to let Mrs. Bellamy continue to think I was my twin sister. I made my decision. Billy and Tommy's enthusiasm really clinched the deal. They would have been so disappointed if I muffed it. I had them to consider as well as myself.

I went through a lot of agony before school ended the following day, but there was no turning back now. I'd thought of putting the whole thing in the Lord's hands. But I was afraid if I did, I'd end up telling the truth, and there would go my dog.

Let's get it over with quick, I thought. I hurried to Mrs. Bellamy's house and rang the bell. Again she answered immediately. I stepped inside the door.

She was still not smiling. She had that strange frown on her face again. "Well, Jennifer? What did your folks say? Do you get to keep Flower? Or should I look for another applicant?"

That's when I knew I couldn't lie. I couldn't bear to have her call me Jennifer. I had to set her straight. I wanted Flower more than anything in the world, and I hated to disappoint Billy and Tommy, but I had to live with myself.

Way deep down I knew that my brothers had nothing to do with my decision. I was just using them to persuade myself to do something wrong. "I'm sorry, Mrs. Bellamy," I blurted. "But I'm not the one who took care of Flower before. I'm Penny, Jennifer's sister." There! I'd said it! I'd blown the whole thing. But somehow I felt good.

She looked at me closely, peering into my face. Finally she spoke. "Yes, I guess my vision is worse than I thought. Anyway, what difference does it make which sister you are as long as you want Flower and you're able to give her a good home?"

"Oh, I can, Mrs. Bellamy. My whole family is excited about it. And Mom and Dad said it's OK. And Jennifer thinks it's great for me to have her. Jenny isn't a dog lover, Mrs. Bellamy. She's responsible, and she'd do a good job. But I'm the one who loves dogs."

"I'm sorry I didn't recognize you at first, Penny." The woman sighed. "I'm having trouble with my eyes. My doctor says I have cataracts, but I keep resisting surgery."

"That's OK," I said. "My sister and I do look a little bit alike. We're twins."

Mrs. Bellamy smiled broadly. "Well, that explains it. I'd seen you talking to Flower every day for so long that when your sister came by that day, I thought it was you. Still, she didn't really take to Flower the way a real dog lover should."

My heart was singing. Here I'd been fighting the truth for a whole day. Now everything was out in the open, and I felt like a free person. And I was still getting to keep Flower as my very own. And poor Mrs. Bellamy. No wonder she had been frowning. She couldn't see!

"Well, enough of this," Mrs. Bellamy said. "Let's go tell Flower who her new mistress is to be."

She led the way through the kitchen, holding onto my arm for guidance as we walked down the steps to the backyard.

LET'S THINK ABOUT IT

1. Have you ever wanted anything so badly that you might have lied to get it? If you had, would you have been happy getting it?
2. If Penny had confided in her mother, what do you think Mrs. Renquist might have said?
3. Have you ever had that feeling of freedom that comes when you have battled with a possible lie and finally decided to tell the truth?
4. Would you want to turn over an important responsibility to someone who had lied to you?
5. Do you think Penny might have saved herself a lot of grief if she had put her problem in the Lord's hands as she had thought about doing?
6. How do you think Jesus would have helped her solve her problem?

◆　◆　◆

Dear God, sometimes a lie comes to my mind so quickly, it seems easier than the truth—particularly if the lie happens to suit my purposes. Please keep me from lying, Lord, that I may walk in your footsteps.

Best Friends

"Honor your father and your mother."

Exodus 20:12

♦   ♦   ♦

It wasn't often that a girl as exciting as Elgin Peterson came to live in Japonica. Then Elgin chose Hilary Lawson to be her best friend. What more could a girl want?

♦   ♦   ♦

I was backing my bicycle out of the rack at school when I heard a voice beside me. I looked up. It was Elgin Peterson.

"Riding my way?" she asked. "Let's ride together."

The invitation sent a warm glow through me. Elgin was new in Japonica. She'd been living here only three months and was already the most popular girl in school.

"Where do you live?" I asked.

She shrugged. "What difference does it make? Ride my way and find out."

I hesitated.

Her eyes narrowed with promise. "It's up to you," she teased. "Do you want to have fun or don't you?"

Ever since first grade my mother had told me to come home from school first and visit with my friends later. I looked at Elgin sheepishly. "I'm supposed to go straight home," I said.

"Do you always do what you're supposed to?" Elgin lifted her little pointed chin.

I shrugged just the way she had, trying to look cool like her. "Not always."

Hopping on our bikes, we started toward the front walk, riding side by side. I grinned, knowing that everyone would see us together, talking and laughing like friends, our feet on the pedals moving in the same rhythm. To be chosen by Elgin was exciting!

Actually she was best friends with Cecily Adams. For weeks, they'd been riding home together every day, eating lunch together, dropping notes in each other's lockers. But Cecily had been absent for several days, and I felt lucky to be right there when Elgin needed someone to ride with.

So when we got to the corner where we should have parted, I went on with her, not waiting to be asked again. She smiled at me, pleased, and I grinned again.

When I finally *did* turn off, two blocks later, Elgin stopped me, looked deeply into my eyes, and said, "Let me tell you something, Hilary. You don't ever have to do anything you don't want to. Remember that."

My mother was in the kitchen when I came in. "Hi there, Hilary. I'm out here. Come on back."

I left my books on the dining room table, grabbed a Golden Delicious from the bowl and joined her. The apple would be a good distraction in case Mom asked too many questions. But apparently I wasn't late enough for her to notice. I breathed a sigh of relief.

"How was school?" Mom asked.

"OK, I guess. Just school." I looked away.

"Anything new happen?"

I took a huge bite of the apple. Busying myself with the juice squirting out of the sides of my mouth, I avoided her eyes as I wiped off the juice with the back of my hand.

"No. Just the usual." I wondered if she knew. But that wasn't Mom's way. She would've asked right out. I grinned at her, happy to be off the hook.

"I got an *A* on the paper I wrote last week," I said.

"That's good. How'd you do on your math homework?"

"I got an *A* on that too." I always made pretty good grades in school, and I knew my parents were proud of me.

The following day, Elgin managed to stand next to me when it was our turn to write on the chalkboard. This was one of Ms. Rhodes' favorite assignments. She'd have us memorize some stanza from a poem. Then she'd call off names of half a dozen kids to write the stanza on the board from memory.

"I didn't study it," Elgin whispered. I could see her copying from what I was writing. Ms. Rhodes said giving help was cheating the same as taking help from another student.

What a foolish rule that is, I decided. What difference did it make if you helped someone? It was the same with coming home from school before going somewhere with friends. *I* knew where I was. Why did my mother have to know too? I could take care of myself.

Later in math class when Mr. Morgan wasn't looking, Elgin passed me a note. Several kids looked at me enviously.

"We'll eat lunch together," the note said.

I was thrilled! To be chosen by Elgin as her best friend was incredible. Well, maybe not her *best* friend. After all, Cecily Adams was Elgin's best friend, and Cecily was back in school that day.

But when lunchtime came, somehow Cecily got the message that she and Elgin were no longer a twosome. Of course I got the message too: Now *I* was Elgin's best friend.

I even found myself using some of her mannerisms, tossing my head in that cool way, joking with some of the boys who joined us at lunch, and sneering at the ones I didn't like.

This went on for several days, and I loved it. We giggled together. We whispered secrets to one another. I felt more important than I'd ever felt in my life. Every day I'd ride as far as her corner, three blocks out of my way, and Mom never found out. One afternoon when we got to the spot where we usually parted, Elgin said, "Come to my house."

"I can't," I told her. "I have to go home first."

Her eyebrows shot up with surprise. "Hilary! You're twelve years old!" She looked at me scornfully. "What did I tell you the other day? Do you remember? You don't have to do anything you don't want to."

"Well, today, I *have* my piano lesson." I said, carefully avoiding the phrase, *have to*. That was a lie. I didn't take piano lessons.

"Well, come tomorrow then."

"I'll ask my mother," I said.

Elgin shook her head in exasperation. "Hilary, you need a lot of education. Don't ask. Just do it. Look. You ask her and she says no. So what do you do? You obey and miss out on a lot of fun. You do it anyway, and she never finds out."

Digesting this kind of thinking was hard for me at first, but it was becoming easier every day.

"And suppose she *does* find out." Elgin laughed. "What's she going to do to you? Kill you?"

There was a long pause. My mind was spinning.

"Why does your mother want you to come home first?" she went on. "For no good reason I can think of except to show you she's in control. It's high time you took control yourself. You know what's good for you. She doesn't. Tomorrow you will come home with me. We'll play CDs and stuff. My mom will be gone."

I wondered if Elgin was right. I was nearly thirteen, about time I began making my own decisions.

"Mom," I said later, "I met this really nice girl at school, and she asked me to come home with her tomorrow after school."

"Who is she, Hilary?"

"Her name is Elgin Peterson. She lives on Pelican Avenue about three blocks from here. Maybe we'll study together." The last was my own idea.

"Does she go to our church?" Mom asked.

"I don't know. I thought I'd invite her for this Sunday."

I could see Mom thinking it over. Finally she said, "I don't see why not. You may go for an hour. We'll see how it works out."

The next day I didn't tell Elgin I'd asked permission. I merely said I'd come.

"Good," she replied, patting my shoulder. "You've got to take things in your own hands. I learned a long time ago that was the only way to handle my mother."

On the way home that afternoon when we passed the little doughnut shop on Chestnut Street, Elgin noticed the Cloverbloom Dairy truck parked outside. "How would you like some ice cream?" she asked.

"Great!" I hadn't planned on going someplace else, but why not?

A wonderful sense of freedom surged through my veins. *This* was living!

"I know the driver. His name is Mel. He'll give you a free ice-cream cone if you kiss him."

He sounded like my grandfather. Gramps was always kissing me and my cousins and bringing us presents.

But Mel wasn't like Gramps at all. He was more the age of my dad.

"Well, there's my little sweetheart," he said when he saw Elgin. "And here's another little sweetheart. You girls want some ice cream? The treat's on me." But before I knew what had happened, he'd grabbed ahold of me and was planting a horrible kiss on my mouth with his awful hands on my body.

Horrified, I pulled away and ran. I could hear Elgin calling, but I didn't look back.

My heart pounded. I didn't even know where I was heading. I felt dirty and frightened and scared of what my mother would do to me. But most of all I felt ashamed and guilty.

When I got to the public library, I was crying. My mother wasn't expecting me for nearly an hour, so I darted inside, found the ladies room, locked myself in one of the stalls, and just sobbed. I kept gagging as if I might throw up. Finally I came out of the stall, washed my face, and rinsed my mouth over and over. Then I found a table away from other people and sat down, pretending to read. In a way the worst part was knowing I had to go home and tell my mother. Elgin would have said, "Why bother telling her?" But by then I knew that if that's what Elgin would advise, then I should do the opposite. In the short time we'd been friends, I'd learned to lie, cheat, deceive my mother, and now this.

How could I have ever thought she was fun? How could I have even liked her? She'd done nothing but get me into trouble, and everything she'd ever said to me was false.

But, from a tiny corner in the back of my mind, I remembered something she told me that *was* true. It was as if I could hear her voice the first day I biked home with her. Those deep brown eyes looked into mine and she said, "Remember, Hilary, you don't ever have to do anything you don't want to."

Then I knew that blaming her was wrong. I was responsible for my own actions. Everything I did was because I wanted to. Nobody made me. I did it all of my own free will.

Suddenly I remembered my bike. I'd left it leaning against the wall of the doughnut shop. When I got there, the dairy truck was gone. So was Elgin's bike. I heaved a sigh of relief.

Thinking through all that happened, I slowly rode home to face my mother.

LET'S TALK ABOUT IT

1. Do you think kids your age should have to ask permission to go home with friends after school?
2. If someone you really liked asked you to do something that you knew was wrong, how hard would it be for you to say no?
3. Since Elgin dumped Cecily so easily, shouldn't Hilary have wondered how loyal a person Elgin was?
4. Do you think Hilary should have gone home and told her mother what happened? What would you do if the same thing happened to you?
5. Would you agree if some stranger asked to take your picture? Would you go for a ride with him if he asked?
6. What are some of the things you'd feel right about saying no to?

◆　◆　◆

Sometimes, God, the wrong people can be so appealing that I'd do almost anything to get in good with them. Instead of letting the wrong person pull me down, please teach me how to pull them up to know you and to love you as I do.

When Pride Gets in the Way

"For by the grace given me I say to every one of you: Do not think of yourself more highly than you ought, but rather think of yourself with sober judgment, in accordance with the measure of faith God has given you." Romans 12:3

◆ ◆ ◆

Nora Voegle thought of herself as pretty special. She had talent, sophistication, and . . . then she met some people who showed her what being special really meant.

◆ ◆ ◆

"This summer, Nora," Aunt Alice said to me one night when she and Uncle Luke were over to dinner, "I want you to help out at the Home."

We have this nursing home in Japonica, and my aunt is the director.

"What can *I* do?" I asked. "I'm only twelve years old." I made a face. *I don't even like old people*, I said to myself. I'm the oldest one in our crowd, and I like that. That makes me feel mature and special.

"You can do plenty," Aunt Alice replied. "Greta Wilson's coming over three mornings a week to give art lessons, and you can help."

"Art lessons! To all those old people? How can they learn anything new?"

Aunt Alice smiled knowingly. "It's not a matter of learning, but—"

"You'd be surprised, Nora," Dad interrupted. "I know folks in their eighties who are pretty spry." Dad owns a used-car lot and knows practically everybody in Japonica.

"But what about my swimming?" I protested. I was on the swim team at our community pool. Charlotte, our coach, demanded that we be there every day. I sure couldn't see myself giving up the team to work with a bunch of dumb *old* people.

"You can swim in the afternoon," Mom said in her that-settles-it voice. "I'm sure Charlotte will understand."

Well, maybe *she* was sure, but I wasn't. I'd never asked to be excused before, and I wasn't going to start now. I'm not the swimmer Babe Remberton is, but I'm pretty good, and I love being on the team.

Actually, I liked the idea of working with Miss Greta. If things had been different, I'd have jumped at the chance to be her assistant. She's the art teacher at Japonica Junior High School where I'll be going next year. And once, when she saw my stuff on display in grade school, she told my mom I had talent.

I think I have talent, too, but it wasn't *me* who'd be getting the teaching. I'd be some kind of "gopher"—go for this, go for that, wash the brushes, carry the water, scrub up the spills.

You know what family pressure is, though, and I ended up doing as I was told. Even Charlotte agreed, and in a way, I felt she'd let me down.

So—on the first Monday of summer vacation, when everyone else was traipsing happily off to the pool, where was I? In this big room at the nursing home out on Military Road, listening to Miss Greta explain the fundamentals of color.

What a bore! There must have been about twenty-five in the class—both men and women. I looked them over as they trickled into the room. Some limped, one old lady came in a wheelchair, and a few carried canes. I sat up front, almost like a teacher, myself, while Miss Greta gave a little lecture on the color wheel.

Right in the front row sat an old man who looked about two hundred. At first he pretended to listen. But pretty soon his head was nodding, his eyes closed, and I could hear him snoring. His name was Mr. O'Connor, according to the name tag he wore.

Behind him in a red-and-white checked dress, a fat old lady, Mrs. Watson, doodled on her pad. Another old lady named Mrs. Ricardo was mending the fingers of a glove. One or two of them took notes and looked almost alive, but on the whole they seemed bored. I wondered why they took the class in the first place. Unless someone in charge was making them go like they make us take certain courses in school.

To tell you the truth, as good an artist as I am, I found it tedious myself. I kept hoping Miss Greta would stop yakking before I spaced out completely.

Bor-r-r-ing—primary colors, secondary colors, how to mix red and blue to get purple—blah, blah, blah.

"We'll start with a still life." Miss Greta finally said. She split open a watermelon, put one slice on a plate, and arranged the rest on a green cloth, artistically draped for the right effect.

"When we're through," she announced, "we'll all eat the watermelon."

Everyone laughed. Well, at least I'll have *something* to look forward to, I thought.

The color scheme was terrific—the dark green of the rind against the pale green cloth, the rich red of the pulp, and all of it accented by the shiny black seeds. My hands itched for a brush. I wished I could have been painting it myself. Instead, I trudged around the room following Miss Greta's orders.

Everyone looked wide awake now as they made their sketches. The room hummed with the sound of busy people. As I went about the jobs Miss Greta had given me to do, I couldn't help but think about the stuff our pastor had talked about the week before.

Like how we could serve the Lord by serving other people: "Whatever you did for one of the least of these brothers of mine, you did for me" (Matthew 25:40). *These funny old people were certainly the least of practically anybody's brothers*, I thought. I was beginning to feel pretty cool, doing something for God. Important too, almost like I was the teacher myself. I guessed that Miss Greta felt the same way. I could hear her voice in the background. "Very good, Mr. O'Connor." "Excellent, Mrs. Watson."

She's a good Christian too, I thought, *just like me. Making those silly old people feel good.*

Miss Greta had introduced me as her assistant at the start of the class and I was beginning to like feeling so important. They'd caught my name from the beginning, and it was "Nora, this," and "Nora, that." I didn't mind too much washing brushes, fetching paint, passing out sheets of paper.

I didn't have time—running here and there—to get a really good look at their work. And what I did see were just a few rough lines. But what they produced didn't matter. I was doing something for the Lord.

The two hours flew by, and before I knew it, Mom was parking the car at the front gate.

"You'd better run, Nora," Miss Greta said. She knew Mom had to get home fast to fix lunch for my dad. "Thank you very much."

All the old people called out to me. "Thank you, Nora. See you Wednesday."

And off I went without even a piece of watermelon.

Well, Wednesday was the day I got the shock of my life. Mom dropped me off early, and when I went up to the art room, I found all of Monday's work on display. The paintings were completed now—vivid, colorful, and all so different.

"Well, what do you think?" Miss Greta asked.

I stopped short. "Hey! Neat!"

"So you think they're good."

"Some of them are fantastic. But I thought—"

"You thought they were just dumb old people hunting for some way to kill time. Sure, they're older, but some of these people have been in my class for years. And some were well-known artists in their time. You remember Mrs. Watson? She was a famous sculptor in Sante Fe before she broke her hip and had to retire. She made a career depicting the lives of Native Americans in New Mexico."

"Is this Mr. O'Connor's painting?" I stared in awe.

"He was one of the finest cartoonists on the staff at *The Times Picayune* in New Orleans. That was all a long time ago. Now they're incapacitated and need help. Even the best of us sometimes end up in a nursing home." She told me about a few of the others. Some couldn't paint at all a few years before but they had learned in her class.

"Mostly, they're just people who've never had a chance to study art before. That's why they took the course." She straightened a picture on the wall. "And that's why I offer this painting class every summer. It may be that we'll unearth some real talent. Also, I thought you could learn something about art yourself from watching these talented people at work."

I'd learned something about art, all right. But even more, I'd learned something about me. My pride had gotten in my way. Of course some had slept during the lesson on the color wheel. Miss Greta had to give it for the beginners. But among all those talented people, I was the only one who thought I was too good for the elementary lesson. I was putting myself above other people.

Old smart aleck me—so smug, and so dumb. I thought *I* was doing the giving when in reality, the least of my brothers was really me.

LET'S TALK ABOUT IT

1. Do you have some special talent that makes you feel superior?
2. Do you know any elderly people? Do you know anyone who lives in a nursing home?
3. Have you ever thought of what it would feel like to be old and to have your activities restricted? Or do you feel, deep inside, that you will always be young and attractive?
4. Do you believe that as people age, they need less in the way of friends or entertainment?
5. Where in the Bible are there instances where Jesus was compassionate to people who were elderly or weak?
6. What else do you think Nora learned from her experiences at the nursing home that isn't mentioned in the story?

◆　◆　◆

Dear Lord Jesus, if some older people seem slow and dumb, please make me realize that once they were young and vivacious too. Remind me that some day I, too, may be older and slower and I will need understanding and companionship.

I Can't Stand My Sister

"How great is the love the Father has lavished on us, that we should be called children of God! And that is what we are!"   1 John 3:1

◆   ◆   ◆

Jennifer Renquist was convinced that her twin sister, Penny, had all the good things in life, and that she was nothing until. . . .

◆   ◆   ◆

A lot of people think twins look exactly alike, but we don't always. At least my twin sister, Penny, and I certainly don't.

I'm Jennifer, and Penny and I are the only twelve-year-old twins in Japonica.

We're the same build, and from a distance each of us could pass for the other. But up close you can sure tell the difference. She has pale gold hair as soft as the silk from a fresh ear of corn, and I have plain old light brown hair like Mom's.

Penny inherited all the good stuff from our parents—the looks, the brains, and the personality. All I got was a strong back. She bubbles and sparkles all the time. I'd like to be vivacious like that, but by the time I think of something to say, everyone's talking about something else. So I come on like a fifty-pound bowling ball.

She gets everything she wants while I have to work and plead to get anything. Like her getting Flower from Mrs. Bellamy last week. All she has to do is put on that little mournful face, and my parents knock themselves out to give her what she wants.

"Of course, you can keep her, darling," Mom said, squeezing her hand. "You've wanted a dog for years. Now you'll have one."

I'll bet if I'd been asking to have a dog, it would have been entirely different. They'd have asked a million questions and ended up saying no anyway. But Penny doesn't even have to pay for Flower's food.

"You take care of her, honey," Daddy said. "Keep the yard clean, and we'll get her food when we buy groceries."

Penny's the popular one, and I'm the tag along. But going places because my precious sister isn't allowed to go without me doesn't make me feel great, either. I can tell you that.

So when Jill Copeland and Cecily Adams told me about Nora Voegle's birthday party, I knew I'd get invited. But I also knew it was just because Penny was getting invited.

"Are you guys going?" I asked Jill.

"Sure. Everyone is. It's going to be boy-girl this year."

When I got home, the mail was on the hall table. There it was—one invitation. *Penny Renquist*, it said on the envelope. That was it. Nothing for me.

I felt like all my insides had been scooped out. I could feel the tears coming to my eyes. To be left out completely felt awful—much worse than being asked because they wanted Penny.

I left the rest of the mail on the hall table and carried Penny's invitation up to my room. I kept looking at it, hoping I'd just missed my name. But it wasn't there no matter how hard I stared at Penny's name.

I heard Mom's car drive up. Almost immediately Penny came bursting in, sounding like she owned the world. You can always tell when Penny's home by all the excitement. Why am I the only dummy in the family?

When I heard her come up the stairs, I grabbed her invitation and jammed it in the back of my dresser.

"Hey, Jennifer, did we get our invitation to Nora's birthday party?"

I looked away. "If anything came, I didn't see it. I think Tommy took in the mail."

"That's weird. Tracy and Bonita already got theirs. Are you sure?" She went outside to check.

All Penny talked about that night at dinner was the party. She was really spaced out about not getting her invitation although she didn't for one minute think she wouldn't be invited.

"Don't worry about it, Honey," Mom said. "It'll come."

But of course the next day it didn't come either. Naturally, it didn't come. I still had it hidden away. My problem was that mine hadn't come either. That day at school, the party was all anyone had talked about. Nora was absent, or I think Penny might even have asked her about the invitations. That's how sure of herself she was.

That night while everyone was watching television, I slipped upstairs. With my heart in my mouth, I opened Penny's invitation. I had some kind of crazy hope that maybe my name was on the inside. But it wasn't. Then—I don't know how I could have done such a thing—I sat there, slowly and deliberately tearing that invitation to bits. I stuffed the shreds back into the envelope, taped it shut, and hid it in the back of my dresser again.

"Do you think we should ask Nora about it?" Penny asked me later as we were getting ready for bed. "I know we're invited, but I'd be happier if I saw it in writing."

I began brushing my hair. "I guess people don't really like us," I replied.

She turned those innocent eyes on me. "Why wouldn't they like us?" I felt really down that night, and I wanted to hurt her as much as I was hurt. "After all," I finally said, "what have we got? We're not rich. We're not all that pretty. And we're not from an important family like Wendy and Babe."

"Nobody thinks about stuff like that in Japonica," Penny replied. But I'd hit a nerve. She suddenly quieted down. A brooding look came over her face. For a moment I thought maybe I shouldn't have said what I did. But then I thought, *Who cares? She needs to be cut down once in a while. She think she's so great.*

The hurt stayed with her for quite a while. After the lights were off, I heard this tiny voice say, "Maybe you're right." It sounded like she was crying.

Just then we heard Mom calling to us as she came up the stairs. "Girls, have you gone to bed yet?"

Mom walked into our room, holding up an envelope. "Daddy just found this in the bushes by the porch. It looks like that invitation you've been waiting for. I imagine Tommy dropped it when he brought in the mail."

We both flicked on our lamps. Mom handed me the envelope, then headed back downstairs. It had my name on it, and it was damp from the evening dew.

"Was there only one?" Penny asked in a hollow voice. She got a sick look on her face. And I had a sick feeling in my stomach.

My mind was racing. I slowly opened the envelope. What should I do? I couldn't tell Penny that I'd torn up her invitation. "That's all right," I said, feeling like an ugly green caterpillar. "Unless you're invited, I won't go either. Who cares about Nora's stupid party?"

"I do," she whispered. She really was crying. My cut had hit the mark.

"Don't cry, Penny. Please. It's no big deal." Then suddenly it all came tumbling out, and I was crying too. "I'm sorry, Penny. You did get an invitation. I tore it up." I rummaged in my dresser and found the envelope with the shredded paper stuffed in it.

"You did what?" I couldn't stand the look she gave me as she grabbed the envelope. Her eyes grew big when she saw what I had done. "I hate you," she screamed. "I hate you." She began throwing the bits of paper in my face, screaming the whole time.

I let her scream. I figured she had a right to be mad.

Then suddenly I was screaming. "You can yell all you want, but you don't know what it's like to be me. You're pretty and you're popular and you're talented. But I'm nothing. I'm tired of being ugly and dumb. I'm tired of being nothing but your twin sister."

I was glad they had the television on downstairs, or Mom would have been up there yelling, herself, at the way we were yelling. Anyway my last remark brought Penny around. She stopped screaming and looked at me as if she'd never seen me before. As she reached for a tissue, she was still crying a little, and so was I.

"All that stuff you were screeching about," she managed to say after she blew her nose, "that's the way I feel. That you inherited all the good stuff, and I got nothing. And the way you act, I can't stand it— so calm, like you're above everyone else. Always looking down your nose at everyone."

"I'm not looking down my nose," I defended hotly. "I'm shy. I never know what to say. And you're so witty! People have fun when they're with you."

"People *feel good* when they're with *you*," Penny shot back. "Once I heard Hilary's mother say, 'I love Jennifer's dignity. She seems to have no trouble growing up at all.' I almost hated you when I heard that. Like you were so superior."

"I don't feel superior," I shouted. "I'd give anything to be quick and witty like you."

"I'm not witty, either. I just run off at the mouth when I'm nervous. No one pays attention anyway. You may not talk much, but when you do, people listen."

We'd both been kneeling on our beds screaming at each other but suddenly she got up and stood in front of the mirror. She ran her fingers through her hair. "If I had that smooth, brown hair like you and Mom, I could have 'dignity' too." She made a face when she used the word, *dignity*. We'd both stopped crying, and I got up and stood next to her. We glared at each other in the mirror.

"But you've got those dimples," I sneered, "and, man, do you use them!"

"I didn't even know I had them," she spat. "But you sure know how to use that stuck-up chin of yours."

"What about your peaches-and-cream complexion?" I demanded. "I wish I had skin like yours."

"I wish I had eyes like yours. 'Like black velvet,' Daddy said once. He says you're sere-e-ene." She dragged out the word sarcastically.

"What did he say about your eyes?" I taunted.
"Like two dancing flames."

She was about to snap back at me when our eyes met in the mirror. Suddenly we were laughing.

"Maybe between the two of us, we'd make one pretty girl," she said.

"Maybe between the two of us, we should be more grateful for the stuff we do have." I felt embarrassed. "God has really been good to us, Penny. I don't know why either of us should be jealous." As we settled down to sleep, I realized how awful I'd been, giving in to temptation, destroying her invitation, allowing jealousy to create that terrible feeling between us.

My last thought before I fell asleep that night was to ask God's forgiveness. And I prayed for strength never to let that kind of thing happen again.

LET'S TALK ABOUT IT

1. Do you ever feel unsure of yourself the way Jennifer did? Do you think you might be blinded to some of your good points?
2. What do you think some of your good points are? Your weak points?
3. How do you think lack of self-assurance might cause you to hurt other people?
4. Do you ever find yourself talking too much, the way Penny did, to cover up an uncomfortable moment?
5. Which of God's commandments covers the problem that the twins had?
6. Was Jennifer right in admitting to Penny what she had done? Do you think it's wrong to become angry once in a while?

◆　◆　◆

Dear God, it's so easy to be jealous of people who you think have everything, especially when it's your own sister and you think you have nothing. Still, Lord, I know you gave us all good points. Help me learn how to look for mine. And please, don't let me have such a vicious fight with my sister ever again.

Spying on the Neighbors

"Do not judge, or you too will be judged. . . . Why do you look at the speck of sawdust in your brother's eye and pay no attention to the plank in your own eye?" Matthew 7:1, 3

◆　◆　◆

It was exciting when a new family moved in next door. But it was a little scary too, as Jill Copeland found out.

◆　◆　◆

Ordinarily Japonica is a peaceable little town. But this fall things went kind of crazy.

Dad had let some weird-looking people pull their trailer into the big lot he owned next to our house, and a lot of people were as mad as a swarm of bees.

81

At first, there were some phone complaints but nothing really scary. And I ought to know because I'm the one who answers the phone. I'm Jill Copeland, "the kid with the vivid imagination," the teachers tell my parents. But when a few threatening calls came in, that frightened even me.

"They're Gypsies, Bob," Mr. Joe Lawson told my dad one night. Mr. Lawson is Hilary's father. He's also Vice President of the First National Bank of Japonica, and his opinion carries weight.

My father is one of only three dentists in town, so his opinion is important too.

"So what?" Dad asked. "I know they're Gypsies."

"People are worried. Something could happen."

I was just twelve years old that summer and curious as a kitten in a room full of mirrors. So I was eavesdropping on their conversation.

"Look, Joe," Dad said, "I've got nothing against Gypsies. The guy paid his rent, they're not disturbing the peace, and I say they stay. It happens to be *my* land."

"The guy has no job," Mr. Lawson argued. "What's he living on? Where'd he get that big black Cadillac?"

"He's a tinsmith. He does bodywork on cars."

"Yeah. Sam Colenko said the guy approached him in the parking lot of the Master Food Store. Offered to bang out the dents in his car right there in the parking lot."

"And—?"

"Sam said, 'No thanks.' You think Sam would fall for that kind of rip-off?"

"Sam's a Christian," Dad reminded. "He might have done better offering him a job in his hardware store."

"No way. You open up your possessions to a guy like that, and you're lucky if you even *have* a store the next day."

Later when I asked Dad about Gypsies, he told me they were people who migrated to Europe from India around 700 years ago. They're nomads. That means they never settle down, which is probably why people don't trust them. Some people figure that since Gypsies have no permanent address, they must be evading the police. *Evading*. I got that word from Dad. Anyway, Dad said there's no more crime among Gypsies than among the rest of the population.

So one afternoon when I saw them pull their car in under the pine trees, I decided to watch what happened from our tree house. If they were planning a murder or a big heist or something, I'd be ready to alert my folks. I picked up a notebook, a pencil, an apple, and a peanut butter sandwich.

If I was going to stake out these people all afternoon, I didn't want to go hungry. Dad and Ted had built steps in the branches, so even carrying all that stuff, I climbed up as easily as riding the escalator in Martin's Department Store.

Ted's my brother—one year older than I am and ten years dumber. You know why I say dumber? Because here were his new binoculars—left where they could be stolen, broken, or rained on. And with such crummy people around, you had to be extra careful. The binoculars came in handy, though, because I could watch what was going on. But the place was as quiet as a spider spinning a web—except for some sheets flapping in the breeze.

I was about to give up when a lady came around from the side of the trailer, set up a chair, and then carried out a little kid—a girl about six.

Watching through the binoculars was fantastic— as clear as if they were two feet away instead of a hundred. And these people were weird. The lady wore a purple-and-orange flowered skirt almost down to her ankles and a big red sweater. They both had long, black hair as straight as the railroad tracks at Howell's Junction. Their eyes were as black as ripe olives.

Then I noticed that the kid had a brace on her leg.

The lady covered her with a bright, striped scarf and went back inside.

I slung Ted's field glasses over my shoulder and climbed down from the tree. Then I walked over to the other lot. Not fast. Just like I didn't know anyone was there. My father owned that land. Why *shouldn't* I roam around it if I pleased? But somehow I knew I was doing wrong. I felt like I was stealing chickens.

When I stood practically on top of the little kid, I acted as if I'd just noticed her for the first time. "Oh. Hi!" I said.

She backed away when I spoke, so I said, "My name's Jill. What's yours?"

"Maria." She eyed the binoculars. "What's that?" She pointed to them.

84

"They're field glasses." I put them in her hands, and she held them up to her eyes. "Turn this little knob until everything's clear." I leaned over to help her. Actually, she was kind of cute. "See?" I took her hand and showed her how to twist the knob.

Suddenly her face lit up. She had the glasses in focus.

"Ooooooh! It's beautiful! Everything's so big!"

"Now turn it and look through the other end. See?" I watched her while she did it. "Now turn the knob."

She giggled. "Now everything's miles away." She trained them all over both yards, looking at everything in detail. Watching her up close, I decided she didn't seem as grubby as she did from a distance.

"Could I have it?" she asked.

"They're not mine," I said. "They belong to my brother." I wished I could have given them to her. You know, her having that bad leg and all. It made me feel sorry for her and grateful that Ted and I weren't handicapped.

"I wish I could have them," she said.

I'd never seen a kid so taken with anything, so when my mom called, I decided to leave them with her until the following day.

That night the most terrible thing happened. Some men who lived on the outskirts of town came to see my father and demanded that he make the Gypsies leave. Dad told me to go to my room, but I could still hear part of their conversation.

"Just send them packing, Dr. Copeland," one of them shouted.

I could hear my father answer, but I couldn't make out any words. Then more shouting. A real snarl. "Just get 'em out, that's all. Maybe they haven't caused any trouble yet, but it's only a matter of time."

"We're a peaceable town," one of the men hollered, "and we don't need any riffraff to come in here and start trouble."

"We're all patients of yours, Doc," another one yelled, "And we don't expect you to take the part of no worthless Gypsies against your own town folk."

"They're the missionaries of Satan, as God is my Witness," another one said, "God never said to harbor the devil in our midst."

There was a lot more shouting, and afterward Dad told them he had no intention of asking the Gypsies to leave. "I don't care how different a person looks," he said. "Maybe we look different to them. God doesn't judge us on appearances, and I'm not going to judge them."

Dad was really mad that night, but the thing that worried me more was that I'd left the binoculars with the little girl, and Dad had told us both we were to stay away. When I thought about it, I felt as if I'd been punched in the stomach. How was I going to get the binoculars back? Maybe these people weren't as honest as Dad thought. Maybe Ted would never see his field glasses again. It would be my fault.

That night after midnight, we all woke to the sound of gunshots. I jumped up and ran into my parents' room trembling. Dad had already hopped out of bed and raced outdoors.

Mom opened her arms, and I climbed into bed with her. When Dad returned, Mom and I were hunched up under the blankets, and Ted was leaning out of the window.

"Just a bunch of hot-headed troublemakers," Dad said, "shooting into the air to frighten the Gypsies."

"Those poor people," Mom said. "Did you talk to them?"

"No. They didn't turn on their lights. I'll talk to them in the morning. But I'm not asking them to leave."

"It makes me angry to see how people can be so cruel," Mom said. "Don't they know what it means to follow Jesus?"

The next morning when I heard Dad's alarm go off, I got up and followed him to the kitchen. He poured us some orange juice, and we looked out the window. Apparently the Gypsies were more scared than he'd realized. The trailer and the Cadillac were both gone. So were the clothesline, their two big trash cans, and everything else. And with them were Ted's field glasses. Now I was really scared because they were brand-new, and they were my brother's favorite thing. That's when I really began to pray.

If word ever got around town that they'd taken Ted's expensive binoculars, it'd prove Daddy to be wrong—even if I explained that I'd loaned them to the little kid.

Dad got out some cereal and milk, but I was too worried to eat. I felt a kind of clutching in my throat every time I thought of the trouble I was in. I figured it would take me over fourteen years to save the money to replace them. Why do I always do such dumb things? And I'd said that Ted was dumb!

But when Dad went out to get the morning paper, there were the glasses, tucked between the big door and the screen.

"Where in the world did these come from?" Dad asked.

I heaved a sigh of relief. But I felt kind of sad about the nice little girl being chased away. Then I told Dad about leaving the glasses with her, and I guess I'll never understand grown-ups. I thought he'd be mad because I went over there, but he wasn't. He yelled at me about a whole bunch of other stuff, though.

"Going to play with the child was fine," he said. "That's normal and friendly. But not because we own the land. As long as they paid their rent, the yard was theirs, and you were trespassing to wander around it as if you were some kind of overlord."

"But Dad" I tried to explain.

"Also, you had no right to lend your brother's belongings to someone else." Dad continued his lecture. "But the worst thing you did was to spy on the neighbors. Respect for other people's property, Jill, includes respect for their privacy."

I thought this over for a minute. "Gee, Dad, I didn't think of them as neighbors. They were so crummy looking, I figured I'd keep an eye on them in case something happened."

"Isn't that the kind of mentality we were dealing with last night? Hunting for trouble, maybe even wanting trouble, before any emerged? They were our neighbors, Jill, as much as the Renquists or the Lawsons or the Andrewses."

"Yeah. I guess you're right."

Dad grunted. "That famous imagination of yours could get you into real trouble if you don't learn to use it right. Just remember, honey, 'Man's home is his castle,' even if his home is just a trailer. And it doesn't matter what color a person's skin is or what language they speak. God tells us to love our neighbor as ourselves. If you have respect for other people, they'll have respect for you. That's what I was trying to explain to our callers last night—that people have to prove they're dishonest before I'll accuse them."

"It seems to me," I said, "that those men were the real troublemakers."

He laughed. "You're right, Jill. You get the point. But with God's help they'll learn. Now what do you say we thank God for our blessings and scramble up some eggs for breakfast?"

THINK ABOUT IT

1. Do you know anyone who looks different from most of the people in your neighborhood?
2. Have you ever thought about how it would feel to live among people who all looked alike if *you* were the only one who was different?
3. Have you ever heard of the concept that a person is innocent until proven guilty? What do you think that means?
4. How would you feel if you learned that someone was spying on everything you did?
5. Have you ever broken someone else's belongings or loaned them out or borrowed them without permission? Has that kind of thing ever happened to you?
6. Do you think that God judges us by how we look?

◆　　◆　　◆

Lord, I'm aware we can't all look alike, but please help me really see it. Please, I pray, don't ever let me hurt people because their skin color, language, or the shape of their eyes is different from mine.

My Guardian Angel

"Do your best to present yourself to God as one approved, a workman who does not need to be ashamed and who correctly handles the word of truth."   2 Timothy 2:15

◆　◆　◆

It looked as if Tracy Andrews would have to go to summer school. But if she did, she would miss out on a lot of fun her last summer before junior high.

◆　◆　◆

Life isn't easy when you have a mother who's a schoolteacher. Especially for someone as dumb as me. Or is it *I*?

I never remember that kind of stuff, and Mom gets uptight over all those rules that no one even thinks about after they leave school.

I remember when they were getting those youth groups together at church. She drove me out of my skull. She wanted me to sign up for the youth paper.

"I'd like to see you work with young people who lean toward that kind of thing, Tracy," she kept saying. "If you were working with them, you'd learn to write, and you'd love it."

But I knew I wouldn't. When you're in a group like that, you get so fenced in with rules and charters and second-vice-presidents, you don't have time for fun.

Some editor would be assigning me jobs. Write this. Write that. Then they'll rewrite it themselves.

That's why I hate English at school. All teachers think about is commas and hyphens and capital letters. Scratch, scratch, scratch. Spreading red ink all over my paper until sometimes it looks like they'd bled all over it.

And that's how the problem began. Early June, with just a couple weeks of school left, Ms. Washington tells me I'm failing English. I had gotten an interim report back in March, warning me, and Dad had been on my case ever since. But I didn't think she'd really go through with it.

"You need more practice writing, Tracy. And one session in summer school should do it. If you tried junior high now with you inability to write, you'd never make it."

Summer school! If she'd cut me open and wrung out my blood, she couldn't have hurt me more.

I tried to be calm while everything inside of me was in a state of shock. "Why do I have to write?" I asked. "I'm the math type. I want to get into computers. My secretary can do the writing."

Ms. Washington consulted her grade book. "Look. The first three papers of the fall semester—*D*. At least you wrote them. But you had the opportunity to rewrite, and you didn't. You could have raised your grade if you had at least tried. Then, no paper at all in December. That made three *F*s."

I spotted a *C* way down the line. "Look! Here! I got a *C* in March."

"Yes, you did. But that was hardly for writing. Remember? That was observation."

I remembered. We had to look out the window and write down everything we saw.

She closed the book.

"Is there any chance I could make it up without going to summer school?" I asked. Not going to summer camp with my friends would be a disaster. I couldn't bear it.

She looked me straight in the eye. "Yes. All I want to know is that you can write well enough to make it in junior high. If you can write just one substantial paper, something that can prove to me that you'll be able to handle a writing assignment in junior high, I might reconsider." Ms. Washington drummed her fingers on her grade book. "Tracy, your mother's a teacher. She wouldn't expect me to send you on when I knew you couldn't make it."

There it was again: "Your mother's a teacher." That's what I'd heard all my life. I didn't see what difference it made. Maybe they wouldn't have expected so much of me if my mother had been an airline pilot or something.

Ms. Washington looked at her calendar. "I'll give you until next Friday. That's a whole week." And in case I wasn't sufficiently grateful, she added, "I think I'm being very generous giving you another chance."

It would be nice to say I went home, wrote a fabulous paper, and passed. But what really happened was that I decided to be honest and tell my folks exactly the way things were. But I must have pressed all the wrong buttons because they flipped when I told them.

"You're failing because you frittered your time away," my mom scolded. "Go! Go! Go! That's all you think about. Run here. Run there. What were you doing last December when you should have been doing your writing assignments?"

She didn't wait for my answer.

"I'll tell you what you were doing. You were skating. And talking on the phone. And spending the night with Alexis."

Alexis Colenko is my best friend. If I wasted time, she wasted it with me. But somehow she managed to maintain a high *B* average.

"You knew you were failing when you got that interim report," Dad said. "Why didn't you do something about it then?"

Again, I didn't have a chance to answer.

"Well, I'll tell you what we'll do," Mom offered, real pleasant now that she'd gotten the mad out of her system. "Let's forget summer school. You and I will write together. I'll be your teacher. Instead of going to camp, you and I can work on writing. How do you feel about that?"

How did I feel? I felt like my social life was totally over! I had to go to camp. You see, there was this boy—Wendy Weaver's brother, Cullen. He was the first boy I'd ever really liked. And he likes me. He even told me so.

"Hey!" Dad exclaimed. "Your own private tutor! You're lucky, Tracy. It's not everybody who has a teacher for a mother."

"But I can't miss summer camp," I protested. "The kids have it all planned. And I'm on the swim team here at the pool." I thought it better not to mention Cullen.

Dad shook his head. "The pool will have to wait this summer. Your schoolwork is more important than swimming. You don't want to repeat a grade, do you?"

"Honey, once you get the hang of writing, you'll find it's a lot of fun," Mom said. "Maybe I'll get some writing done, myself."

Then the phone rang, and that's the way they left it. But it wasn't the way I left it. I could still write that paper. That was better than anything I'd been offered so far. Even if it took me a whole week of drudgery, I'd rather do that than miss summer camp.

So when Alexis called, I told her I couldn't talk. I settled down at my desk to write, but not one word came out. I sat there with my pencil poised over my notebook until I had to give up. I finally called Alexis, and we talked for an hour.

Where the rest of the weekend went, I don't know. The words just wouldn't come. By Monday, with only four days left, I felt as if my brain was trapped in an iron cage. And little by little a new thought began to creep into my mind. I could always copy something from a book that no one knew about.

It was a terrible thing to consider, but it was the only way. I couldn't repeat a grade. And I couldn't miss summer camp. I *wouldn't* miss summer camp.

But what could I copy? It would have to be something no one could ever trace. I even spent time in the library hunting for some dusty old book on a back shelf that no one had ever heard about.

Then suddenly, I found the answer. Thursday after school I was thumbing through some old magazines when I came across a British publication my aunt had picked up on the plane, returning from England over two years ago. She'd used my room when she stayed with us, and she left the magazine behind.

"Is There a Guardian Angel Watching Over You?" was the name of the article. It didn't have one word in it that I didn't know, and it was just long enough to be considered "substantial." If anyone asked me how I knew all that stuff about Joan of Arc and Winston Churchill, I could always say I researched it. *My own guardian angel was sure watching over me when I found that magazine,* I thought.

It took me three hours, but with my door locked, I copied every word, I watched every comma and every capital letter. Even the semicolons. And when I got through, I had the most perfect paper I could imagine. Even my parents tiptoed around when they found me writing.

"What did you do about that assignment?" Alexis asked when I called her after supper.

"Oh, it's all written," I said airily. "I'm turning it in tomorrow. Right on time!"

"What's it about?" she asked.

"Well . . . it's . . . it's hard to say, Alexis. Don't be so nosy." I could tell I'd hurt her feelings.

"That's not nosy. I'm interested."

"Well, I just don't want to talk about it. I gotta go now," I said quickly, and I hung up.

That's when I began to worry. If I couldn't talk about it to Alexis, who is like another me, how could I talk about it to Ms. Washington?

I felt like Adam and Eve after they ate the forbidden fruit—my insides all squeezed up and my throat so tight I couldn't breathe. That's when I knew I could never turn the paper in as my own. It's what Ms. Washington called plagiarism, and she'd warned us about it.

Suddenly I hated that paper. My whole life was a disaster and all because I hadn't done the work I should have. I could have done it. I'm nobody's dummy. Now I'd fail English, and Cullen would go off to camp without me and find some other girl. I was desperate.

Perhaps if I explained it to Ms. Washington, she'd understand. But I knew I couldn't face her, so I locked my door again and wrote her a letter. It was a letter, so I didn't worry about commas and capital letters. I told her the whole story. Even about Cullen. Even how I almost turned in a paper that wasn't mine.

As I wrote, I began to feel better—as if I could breathe again. I knew now that here was where my guardian angel had really come to my aid, keeping me from cheating. My whole family would have been disgraced if I had done something so awful. I finally finished off with a plea for understanding.

"And so, Ms. Washington, if you can find it in your heart to let me pass so I can go to camp with my friends, I promise I'll work on writing, and I won't disgrace you or my family."

"So you have the paper!" she said when I handed it to her Friday after class.

"No. I don't. It's just a letter." I shoved it in her hand and raced out the door.

When I was leaving my last class—art—my teacher, Mr. Archer, stopped me. "Oh, Tracy, I almost forgot," he said. "Ms. Washington wants to see you."

I was terrified. Why had I told her about almost plagiarizing? In my school, you get expelled for cheating.

But I stopped by her room anyway with a quick prayer on the way over. And I could tell by the look on her face that at least I wasn't in too much trouble. I slithered into a chair in the front row to wait for my lecture.

But the first words that came out of Ms. Washington's mouth were, "Why didn't you write me papers like this all year?"

"I don't know what you mean." I was thinking of all the mistakes I'd made.

"Everything you've ever turned in, until now, has been so stiff it was as if you had to dig the words out of concrete. This writing flows. It has feeling. I could actually sense your pain. But I want to tell you something, Tracy. I'm not a teacher whose heartstrings you can pull. I don't have a merciful nature."

She handed me the paper. It had a big red *C*+ on it. "I'm passing you because I know now that you can write if you don't get paralyzed over rules but just let yourself go."

"Oh, thank you, Ms. Washington."

"Have fun at camp," she said as I left. "And when you get to junior high, *write* with *feeling!*"

LET'S TALK ABOUT IT

1. What would you do if you found yourself about to fail a grade just as Tracy did?
2. Have you ever felt that something was so important that you might have cheated in order to get it?
3. Is there anything in Christ's teachings that would lead you to believe that plagiarism is wrong? Why isn't it the same as research?
4. Do you feel that Tracy's whole family would have felt the disgrace if she had been expelled for cheating?
5. Suppose your sister or brother were to get into trouble, do you think it would affect you?

◆　◆　◆

I am very weak, Lord, and sometimes schoolwork seems like such a drag that I'm tempted to take the easy way out. I need help to stay honest and not to do things that would hurt you and disgrace myself and others.

It All Sounded So Logical

"Be very careful, then, how you live—not as un-
wise but as wise . . . Therefore do not be foolish, but
understand what the Lord's will is." Ephesians 5:15,
17

◆　◆　◆

*Bonita Bentley hoped her plan to interest Susan
and Cheryl in Camp Watoba might bring them closer
to God—until her whole plan backfired.*

◆　◆　◆

I'd just hung up from talking to Cheryl Armstrong
when my best friend, Nora Voegle, phoned.

"Oh, hi, Nora. I was just about to call you. Who
do you think volunteered to be counselor aides?" I

exploded before she even had time to speak. "Cheryl Armstrong and Susan Humphrey!"

I could tell my announcement had made an impact. They were both members of our church, but they hardly ever came.

Cheryl and Susan were two of the most dynamic girls in our class. They were friendly enough, but we traveled in entirely different circles. They were part of the "in" crowd—student council, cheerleaders— all that kind of thing. They even had their own special club—the DELTAS.

"So what happened?" Nora prodded.

"Just that. They want to be aides at camp. They're going to talk to Pastor Blanchard and Mrs. Wallace tomorrow."

Camp Watoba is a Christian camp that most of us have been going to for years, and Mrs. Wallace had asked me to round up a group of kids to serve as aides the first two weeks. We'd get the campground ready one week and then help the counselors the next week.

Until now, Nora, Babe, and Cecily were the only volunteers I'd been able to enlist, although the rest of our crowd would join us later for junior-high week. Now with Cheryl and Susan coming, I felt like a success. This might be just what they needed to bring them closer to God.

Also, becoming friendly with them could open doors for Nora and me. I could just see us next year in school, close friends with all the "in" people.

The next day Cheryl and Susan came to church and even stayed for Sunday school. They got the official OK and by Wednesday morning we were all on our way in Mrs. Wallace's van.

Watoba is only sixty miles from Japonica, and we sailed down the highway like we owned the world. They'd even given me a nickname—Bunny—and I loved it after having been plain old Bonita for so long. When we arrived, Mrs. Wallace told us six aides were to share the two rooms in the Cottage, and the adults would stay in the Big House.

"Work out roommates any way you wish," she said. "And after you're settled, I'd like you to unpack the Bibles and the hymnals. I'll be in the kitchen looking over the equipment there."

Left to ourselves, we lugged our gear over to the Cottage, a small frame building divided into two equal-sized rooms.

When Cheryl saw the identical rooms with three cots, three dressers, and three overstuffed chairs, she laughed. "Looks like the Three Bears' Cottage," she said.

Flopping into one of the chairs, Susan groaned, "This chair is too hard."

Then Cheryl plopped into another. "And this chair is too soft."

Whereupon I sank deeply into the third, sighing. "And this chair is exactly right."

Everybody laughed.

Susan gestured toward Cheryl and me. "Why don't we three take this room and you guys take the other?"

I tried to ignore the hurt look in Nora's eyes. I should have refused Susan's offer and roomed with Nora, but—well, I didn't.

When the others had gone, Cheryl looked at me kind of funny. Then she looked at Susan. Then they both looked at me again. Even though they weren't saying anything, I could tell they were discussing me. It gave me a creepy feeling.

Finally Cheryl said, "Shall we tell her?"

"Sure. Why not?"

"Well. . . ." Cheryl paused. Then she blurted, "We've put your name in for the DELTAS."

"Who, me?" My voice sounded like the squeak of a startled mouse.

Susan laughed. "Yes, you. We've been watching you, Bunny. You look like a lot of fun."

"We haven't voted on you yet," Cheryl explained. "But your name is up for consideration. That's why we wanted to come to camp—so we could get to know you better."

"Gee, that's super!" I said. I couldn't wait to tell Nora.

"Well, it's still a secret," Cheryl warned, "so don't mention it."

My head was spinning. The DELTAS was a secret organization with all kinds of secret rituals and stuff. I unpacked quickly and left for the storeroom where the others would be waiting. Imagine! Me! In the DELTAS! Once I was in, I'd get Nora in, but for the time being, I knew I had to keep quiet about it.

Babe, Nora, Cecily and I got to work quickly. Cheryl and Susan never did show, so the four of us handled the job alone. It wasn't that much work. We had all those Bibles and hymnals unpacked in no time.

"Why don't you girls take a swim before lunch?" Mrs. Wallace suggested, several jobs later. "You've worked all morning, and you must be hot and tired."

My roommates were sleeping when we went back to put on our swimsuits, so I tiptoed around, getting ready. We'd left so early that morning, I decided they must be really tired.

They were awake when we returned from our swim, and everyone went over to the kitchen to help prepare lunch.

We spent the next couple of days doing other chores—opening cabins, pulling mattresses out into the sunshine to air them, and stacking the dishes in the pantry.

In between chores, we had a great time swimming, talking, and eating.

The only problem was Nora. She kept saying Cheryl and Susan were silly. But that was what made them fun. They were full of crazy antics and had us in stitches most of the time. They did duck out of some of the chores, which embarrassed me, but I figured they were tired and needed the rest.

This went on for several days until the day before camp was to open. After policing the grounds in the late-morning sun, the four of us were ready for a dip in the river. When I returned to the room to get ready, my roomies were sitting there giggling. A strange odor filled the room, an odor I'd smelled before but couldn't identify. Suddenly it hit me. It was marijuana!

I don't know how I knew, but I did. I'd heard people talk about that sweetish smell. I felt as if I'd been gouged in the stomach with a pitch fork.

"What's going on?" Cheryl asked. "Is lunch ready yet?"

I couldn't even answer I was so stunned.

Just then Nora called to me from outside the Cottage.

"Go on without me, Nora," I hollered. "I'll be along."

When Nora and the others left, Susan said, "We were about to have another joint. Want a drag?"

I couldn't even answer.

They both laughed.

"She's shocked," Cheryl said with a grin.

"She'll get over it."

"Don't you smoke, really?" Cheryl asked.

"N-no. I don't." I sure didn't want to act like a nerd, but I knew that's what they'd think I was if I didn't handle this right.

"You will. We'll teach you. There's no time like the present."

"I can't do it, Cheryl. I promised my parents—"

"Everybody promises their parents. Don't let a little thing like that bother you."

"But it would. I'm just—"

"You're just scared. Everybody is the first time." She smiled invitingly. "If you're going to be a DELTA, you might as well get used to lots of exciting stuff. DELTAS aren't babies."

Suddenly, she became serious. "Look, Bonita, either you're with us or you aren't. The choice is up to you." Her eyes narrowed. "Maybe you're not DELTA material after all."

"There's nothing wrong with a little grass," Susan put in. "Think of it logically. If there was, do you think we'd do it? We're not stupid, you know." She laughed. "It's a fun thing that grown-ups have banned without knowing one thing about it. Has anybody's parents tried it? How do they know it's so bad? I've been smoking for close to a year, and it hasn't hurt me one bit."

If my head was swimming before, it was drowning now. All kinds of conflicting thoughts flooded my brain. In a way, I was almost convinced. It did sound logical, the way they put it, and I sure didn't want to blow my chance to be in the DELTAS now.

Why not at least try it? I thought. One time couldn't hurt. If I chickened out now, my whole future with the "in" crowd was shot. While they sailed through life in a whirlwind of fun and activity, I'd be plodding along like a big cow.

Yet something held me back. "I've read that if you try marijuana, you're likely to go on to even stronger drugs," I said finally. "Have you ever tried anything stronger?"

Susan shrugged. "Sure. Once or twice. So what?" She stubbed out the joint and tucked the remaining piece in her handbag.

"Aren't you afraid of what it might do to you?" I asked. "Suppose you got into crack."

"What happens to us isn't your responsibility." Cheryl's words stung.

"Think about it," Susan said, turning away. "Come on, Cheryl. Let's get ready to go for a swim."

Suddenly I made up my mind. I couldn't do it. The word *responsibility* got me.

"You must act with responsibility," my father had often told us kids. "Responsibility to yourself and to God as well as to others."

As Susan and Cheryl started putting on their suits, I cleared my throat. I wanted it all over with now. "Look, you guys. You said to think it over. Well, I have. And for me, it's no good. As you said, I'm just not DELTA material."

Susan was impatient. "I don't think you are either. Just stay out of our way, and we'll stay out of yours. Maybe you'd better move in with the other chickens."

"It's not that easy," I said. "You don't belong here at camp. We have little kids coming. We're supposed to be a good example to them. They're our responsibility." Susan glared at me as if I was a black widow spider.

"So what are you telling us? Are you going to tattle?"

"No. You're going to call your folks and have them come pick you up." I surprised myself with my boldness. But the more I said, the easier it got. "I don't care what you tell them. That's up to you. If smoking pot is all that cool, then convince them. Not me."

Their parents came for them that night. And once they were gone, everything cleared up between Nora and me.

But it was frightening how my plan almost backfired. Here, I'd been hoping to influence them, and I almost went under, myself. As my father says, "Sometimes you have to fight just to stay afloat."

LET'S TALK ABOUT IT

1. What do you think of secret organizations? Why do you think they may be secret?
2. If you were ever invited to join a secret society, do you think you would mention it to your parents?
3. How important is a "best" friend to you? Should Bonita have agreed to room with Cheryl and Susan? What would have been a good way to determine who roomed with whom?
4. Why do you think your parents are opposed to the use of illegal drugs?
5. Have you thought about what you would say if someone asked you to try drugs?
6. Where in Scripture does it say not to use mind-altering substances?

◆　◆　◆

Dear Lord, all my life I've been warned that drugs were harmful. Yet it's easy to be tempted when kids tell you how great the stuff is. Please, God, don't let me harm the healthy body and the good brain you gave me.

She Had to Be the Thief

"A friend loves at all times."   Proverbs 17:17

◆   ◆   ◆

*When things started disappearing at camp, Alexis
Colenko was sure she knew who had stolen them.*

◆   ◆   ◆

We had just started our first lesson on the potter's
wheel at Camp Watoba's junior-high week when I
realized what fantastic pictures this activity would
make. I dashed back to our cabin to get my camera.

The trouble was, I couldn't find it. "I thought sure
my camera was here in the cabin," I mumbled to
myself. I'd already rummaged through my suitcase.

Now I searched under my bed. Except for a few rolls of dust, I didn't find anything.

Pushing my suitcase back under the bed, I raced back to the handicraft cabin. *If I don't get back, I won't get to run the wheel myself*, I thought.

"Where've you been, Alexis?" Tracy asked. "You almost missed your turn."

"I was hunting for my camera," I replied. But as I absently watched Babe working on her bit of clay, I forgot all about my camera. Then it was my turn to "throw a pot." It took all my attention to mold that squishy hunk of clay with my fingers as it spun on the wheel. This was the most exciting thing I'd done in a long while, and I really loved it.

When I'd finally done as much as I could and the rotating wheel slowed down, I felt a sudden joy as I looked at my creation. I surveyed it proudly on the plate where it rested. The pot I'd created was just a simple bowl, my first experience with pottery. But, smooth as a teacup, it did have shape—actually a graceful shape.

"Hey, that's neat," Bryan Remberton's voice interrupted my reverie. "You ever do this stuff before?"

I grinned. "No, I'm a natural-born genius."

"My friend, the genius!" He punched me playfully on the arm.

Jill Copeland looked at my bowl with admiration. "But yours really is great. Look at mine. All wobbly and bunchy. I'm jealous."

"All right, kids!" Beth Simpson, a handicraft counselor, got our attention. "Now we'll leave all these priceless works of art right where they are to dry out a bit. We'll get back to them later with the next step."

Then it was swimming time. A bunch of boys and girls were already waiting outside the dining hall for the trek over to the river when Babe and Jill and I raced back to the cabin to put on our swimsuits.

The suits were hanging on the line outside the cabin.

"Where's mine?" Babe asked.

Everyone was so busy changing clothes that no one listened. I could see her, though, looking in her suitcase, on the doorknob, and on the wall hooks.

"Hey, are you guys playing a trick on me?" she asked.

"No one's playing a trick on you," I mimicked. "Maybe it blew off the line. Look around the trees."

Jill went out to help, and I followed. Kicking through the leaves and the underbrush, we made a thorough search. But no suit.

"I know I hung it out here yesterday afternoon," Babe said.

"Looks like everything's disappearing today," I remarked. "I can't find my camera, and now Babe can't find her suit."

"I bet one of those wild pigs got it," Jill suggested.

There were several wild pigs in the woods, and sometimes at night people heard them grunting and sniffing around, searching for food. The year before, they'd made off with Tracy's swimsuit. She found it later—torn to shreds and filthy dirty but completely identifiable.

"Why don't you borrow Penny's suit?" Tracy suggested. "She went home for her cousin's wedding. Remember? She wouldn't mind."

"And you can pick up one the next time we go to town," I said.

And so it was settled. Babe slipped into Penny's suit, and the three of us joined the others at the river. But Horseface, the waterfront counselor, gave us each three demerits for being late.

Later, as a bunch of us climbed the hill together on our way back to camp, I was still pretty angry about the demerits.

"It wasn't your fault, Alexis." Bryan tried to calm me down.

"It sure wasn't," Babe said. "You guys were helping me. I asked Horseface to give all nine demerits to me, but you know how he is."

"Don't worry about it," Jill said. "We'll earn 'em off."

That's a good idea, I thought. The camp staff penalized us for all kinds of stuff, but by doing something positive—like helping someone or going on extra duty—we could cancel out the black marks.

At lunch Horseface asked, "Did anyone see my whistle? I hung it on a tree when I went swimming, and when I came back it was gone."

"Hey! Hey!" Ted Copeland cheered. "That means you can't make us get out of the water now. No whistle, no control."

Horseface grinned. "I've got other ways of control." He arranged his hands as if he were holding a baseball bat and looked menacingly at Ted. They all laughed, but all I could think about was everyone suddenly losing things.

"That's three things that disappeared in one day." I said to the group at my table. "My camera. Babe's swimsuit. Now Horseface's whistle. There's someone in this camp who thinks he's being ver-r-r-y funny."

"Well, I wish he'd cut the comedy soon," Babe mumbled. "I want my swimsuit."

The next day several other things disappeared. Bryan Remberton's book on surfing, several pieces of clothing, and finally a box of Ping-Pong balls was missing from the recreation room.

That afternoon while I was helping Martha hunt for her tiger tee shirt, I reached under Jill's bed and there it was. Or at least the sleeve. It was sticking out of the side of Jill's suitcase where it apparently had been shoved hastily before snapping the lid shut.

Without stopping to think I flipped open the lid. There in Jill's suitcase were all the things that had disappeared. Well, a couple anyway. I slammed the lid shut and pushed the suitcase back where it belonged.

Jill! So Jill was a thief! It didn't surprise me. She'd been so sweet, pretending to help people find things she knew she had. There was only one thing for me to do—tell Mrs. Wallace, the camp director. I decided to leave the evidence right where it was. The more I thought about it, the more I was convinced that Jill was the one who'd stolen all our stuff.

I was tempted to tell Mrs. Wallace right then and there. Still, I hated to get Jill in trouble. Then a bunch of us stopped off at the handicraft cabin to admire our pots, which were still drying out.

Mine was gone! Well, that was too much! I remembered how Jill had admired it. She'd even said she was jealous.

Later, at evening worship, I watched Jill as she sang the hymns. *What a hypocrite!* I thought.

When worship was over, we all headed back to our cabin, but I left the gang and walked over to see Mrs. Wallace.

"That's a serious accusation you're making, Alexis." Mrs. Wallace looked at me gravely. "Did you actually see her take anything?"

"No. But I have all the evidence I need to know I'm right." I told her about my pot and how envious Jill had been. "And when Babe couldn't find her swimsuit," I went on, "Jill was the first to offer to look for it. That was to let us all know how helpful she was, to keep people from suspecting her."

Mrs. Wallace frowned. "And Jill was the one who suggested that the wild pigs might have taken Babe's suit. See what she was doing? Trying to shift suspicion away from herself."

"Did you see your camera in her suitcase?" Mrs. Wallace asked.

"Well, I didn't actually see it. But it could have been under other stuff. And I did see Bryan's surfing book. And I saw Martha's tee shirt that disappeared— the one with the tiger on it."

Mrs. Wallace seemed to be giving it all serious thought. "Tell you what . . ." she said. "Let's go on over to your cabin and talk to Jill herself."

I must have looked shocked because Mrs. Wallace said, "It's the only fair thing to do, Alexis. You should confront Jill openly and let her speak for herself."

Martha greeted us when we got to the cabin. "Hey, I found my sweatshirt," she said. "I forgot I'd loaned it to Jill last night."

"And here's your camera," Bonita said. "Horseface brought it over. He found it down by the river when he went back to hunt for his whistle. You're lucky it hasn't rained recently. He found his whistle too."

I gasped, suddenly remembering that I'd taken some pictures down at the river. Then some kids came along and we started talking and I set my camera down. I had forgotten all about it. "You look shocked," Jill said. "Aren't you glad he found it?"

"Sure, but . . ."

I bit my lip. "I'm sorry. I thought maybe someone here had . . . well, you know."

"Stolen it?" Babe said angrily. "Nobody here would do that."

"Alexis meant no harm, Babe," Jill said kindly. "If that's what she thought, I think she had a lot of courage to tell us. Otherwise everyone would have been under suspicion."

My shame was growing deeper every minute. Here was Jill, the very one I'd suspected, being so understanding.

"What about Bryan's book on surfing?" Mrs. Wallace asked. "Did that show up too?"

Jill looked up innocently. "I have that. Why? Did he forget he loaned it to me?"

"Looks like all the lost articles have been accounted for then, including the Ping-Pong balls."

We looked at her, waiting for an explanation.

She grinned. "I guess I'm forgetful too. I had just bought them, and I thought I had dropped them off in the rec room, but I hadn't. I found them in my car."

"What about my swimsuit?" Babe asked hopefully. "Has that turned up too?"

"No, Babe. I'm sorry. But let's keep looking," I told her. I didn't even mention my pottery. I felt too ashamed.

The next day Beth Simpson returned my bowl to the handicraft cabin while I was there. "It's beautifully done, Alexis. I borrowed it to show that reporter from the paper. He's coming back in a few days to take some pictures. You have a lot of talent."

Unfortunately, Babe's suit was found—ripped to shreds—over by the pump. Apparently the wild pigs really had gotten to it, just as Jill suggested. I don't know where Martha found her tee shirt with the tiger on it, but the next day she had it on, and Jill was wearing hers too. The shirts were identical.

That night when I said my prayers, I asked God to forgive me for being so suspicious. It's hard to imagine how much trouble I might have caused with my accusations.

LET'S THINK ABOUT IT

1. Should Alexis have gone to Mrs. Wallace with her suspicions regarding Jill? Or should she have openly accused Jill of having stolen the missing articles? Or should she have discussed it with several other cabin mates?
2. How else might Alexis have handled her suspicions?
3. Have you ever been absolutely sure about something that you later found to be totally wrong?
4. What would you do if you thought a good friend had stolen something?
5. What would you do if someone accused you of having done something that you hadn't done? Would you be able to forgive that person?
6. Was Alexis guilty of bearing false witness, or was she just guilty of making a rash judgment without having evidence first?

◆ ◆ ◆

Dear God, sometimes I think I know all the answers and jump to conclusions too soon. Wouldn't it be terrible to accuse a friend of something she didn't do? Teach me, Lord, to have patience and to think things through before I go jumping in with both feet.

Walk with Your Head High

"No temptation has seized you except what is common to man. And God is faithful; he will not let you be tempted beyond what you can bear."

1 Corinthians 10:13

◆　◆　◆

Cecily Adams's world seemed to be back on its axis again. Then Elgin Peterson came into her life.

◆　◆　◆

Cecily Adams. I wrote my name neatly at the top of the page and slipped it in my notebook. It was still only 8:00, and Mom said I could watch television for an hour before I went to bed if I had everything ready for school on Monday. I'd always been a good student, but my work had slipped recently, and Mom had been clamping down.

That's when the phone rang. Mom answered it. "Cecily, it's that Elgin girl. You may talk for ten minutes. No longer." She spoke in that grim voice she'd developed ever since she met Elgin.

I knew she didn't like Elgin although she'd never actually said so. Elgin was advanced, and parents never like kids running with people they don't understand. She wore cute clothes and was very witty, but Mom seemed to blame her for my work slipping.

I raced to the phone. I hadn't heard from Elgin in about three weeks.

"Hi," I said. "Elgin?"

"Sure. How you doin'?"

"I'm doing fine. How about you?"

"Bouncy as a red balloon," she answered. Elgin always had such cute things to say. I'd never had a friend like her before, and for a while we'd been really close. Then I got the flu, missed school for a few days, and when I returned, Hilary Lawson had muscled in. I hate her. Acting so cool, copying everything Elgin did. Anyway, I was out and it really hurt.

"You haven't been around lately," Elgin said. "Who've you been hanging out with, anyway?"

I could feel myself shrugging and tossing my head the way she did. "No one—and everyone." I hoped I sounded mysterious and cute.

"Well, it's not nice to ignore your old friends, Cecily. We'll have to get together. How about tomorrow?

Want to hang out for a while at the mall? We can have lunch and try on clothes."

I had to think quick. If I asked my mother, there was no way she would allow me to spend the whole day hanging around the mall. But Mom worked on Saturdays, and I felt sure I could manage it. I had to be careful, though. Even though Mom was sitting in the living room with the TV on, I knew she was listening to every word I uttered.

"Sounds good to me," I said.

"Well, where do you want to meet me?"

"Whatever you think."

"Is the jewelry department at Penney's OK?"

"That's great."

"About ten-thirty?"

"Fine," I said.

"What's the matter? Can't you talk?"

"Not really."

"Yeah. I know what you mean."

I figured I'd better break it off, so I said, "Well, look, Elgin, I gotta go now. I'll see you around."

Mom couldn't wait to jump on me. "You haven't heard from her in a long time. What did she want?"

"Nothing. Just to talk." I figured it would be good to change the subject. "What do you want me to fix for supper tomorrow?"

Mom sighed. "I guess you could thaw some hamburger patties and a couple of English muffins. I wish I didn't have to work on Saturdays. I'd like to be at home with you tomorrow."

I patted her shoulder. "Don't worry about me, Mom. I may get together with Nora or Bonita or someone. What I'd like to do is to buy a pair of shoes at Kinney's. I really need them."

Kinney's is in a little neighborhood shopping center about two blocks away.

"That's OK, Cecily. Just be sure they fit. I'll leave you some money. And don't hang around too long."

When I woke up the next morning, Mom was gone. She'd left me some money for the shoes, plus a five dollar bill for some lunch. So I made my bed, washed the breakfast dishes, and got out fast.

Elgin was waiting, which was unusual. "I've missed you, Cecily. You know when you were sick I found myself trying to be nice to Hilary Lawson, and somehow I got stuck with her. But that girl's a real drag. I finally had to dump her."

"Yeah, I guess she is." Actually, I used to think Hilary was a lot of fun until she double-crossed me with Elgin. That really hurt my feelings. But it felt so good hanging out with Elgin again that Hilary Lawson didn't matter anymore.

We just rolled along having a great time. First we tried on shoes at Walker Sports. I didn't buy any because they cost too much. We tried on jeans, and then we went over to Martin's Department Store and sprayed ourselves with the free Estee Lauder.

After that, we bought some pizza and Cokes and sat on a bench near the fountain and people-watched, making fun of everyone. A lot of kids we knew came along, but I was glad no one tried to horn in.

Finally when we'd eaten all our food, Elgin said, "Let's go over to the Swim and Surf Shop at Ella

May's and see the new swimsuits. Maybe they're having a sale."

Ella May's is a very exclusive shop where everything costs a million dollars.

We went to the Swim and Surf Shop toward the back of the store. The prices shocked me. Summer was here and I needed a new swimsuit bad. But some of these cost twice what they did last year. Some day, I figured, I was going to have a lot of money. Then I could buy anything I wanted, but right now we were anything but rich. And being poor in Japonica Junior High isn't easy. Everybody I hang out with seems to have more money than I have.

Wendy Weaver's dad is a doctor, and Babe Remberton's dad is a lawyer, and Martha Hicks' dad is an architect. But my dad is dead, and Mom supports us all—her, me and my brother, Bud, who's away at college—on her salary as a receptionist at Japonica General Hospital.

"Try this one on," Elgin urged. "You'd look super in it."

I agreed, and we went back to the fitting room. She was right. It was perfect. The fit, the color, the feel—everything.

Elgin stood back and looked at me critically. "It's super! You're a knockout! Buy it!" she ordered.

"I don't have that kind of money, Elgin."

"Didn't you say your mom gave you some money?"

"Sure. But that was for shoes." I was tempted. I looked at myself in the mirror again. I looked fantastic. What would happen, I wondered, if I bought the swimsuit instead? Of course I knew what would happen. Mom would kill me. Still . . . I was turning it over in my mind.

"So she yells at you," Elgin said. "Moms yell anyway. And stores don't take swimsuits back. So once you buy it, you know it's yours. Go on. Call the clerk and tell her you want the suit."

Elgin leaned over with her face real close to mine and whispered, "Or—you could forget to take it off."

"Forget to do what?"

She clapped her hand over my mouth and gave me an angry look. "Shut up!" she hissed.

Then she was whispering again, so quiet it was as if she was mouthing the words instead of actually saying them. "Just forget to take it off." Reaching for my shirt on the floor where I'd dropped it when I undressed, she tried to slip it over my head.

I pushed her away. "No. I can't do that," I whispered.

"Yes, you can. You're just chicken." She got that put-down look on her face that I'd seen her use on other people. Suddenly she was digging in the bottom of that big handbag of hers. "You want to see something?" she whispered. She opened her purse wide. "See?" she said, leaning back so I could peer down into it. There, next to her wallet was a pair of earrings with the price tag still attached. "If I can do it, so can you."

"Solid gold." She was whispering again, mouthing the words. "I picked them up when we first came in. And you didn't even see me."

She zipped up her handbag. "You have to help yourself in this world if you want to get anywhere." She tried to slip my shirt over my head again.

"No!" I said it again. "No!"

"Chicken!" She made an ugly face.

I wanted that swimsuit so bad I ached for it. And I hated being called chicken. I was really tempted.

"Just walk out with your head high," she whispered. "And don't look at anyone."

Just walk with your head high. Those were the words that did it. How could I ever walk with my head high again if I did what she was telling me to do? It was stealing. It was shoplifting. It was a sin, probably the worst sin I'd ever even thought about. And God had been so good to me. Why would I want to hurt God like this?

I pushed her away and began pulling off the suit.

Elgin gathered her things together. "You are one boring baby," she spat. "Chicken!" She flounced out of the fitting room while I was zipping up my jeans.

I followed her through the store, past the blouses and the sweaters and the handbags and the jewelry. I could see her back, as straight as a cue stick, her head high.

As Elgin stepped out the door to the mall, a tall woman in a dark-blue dress reached out and grasped her wrist, murmuring something I couldn't hear.

Elgin turned, and I could see the stricken look on her face.

The woman marched her quietly back through the store, never releasing the grip on her arm.

LET'S TALK ABOUT IT

1. Why do you think Cecily's mother felt safe in giving her money for the shoes? Could you betray that kind of trust?
2. Have you ever wanted something as badly as Cecily wanted that swimsuit?
3. When should Cecily first have sensed that Elgin meant no good and put a stop to the activity in the fitting room?
4. How do you think it would feel to have less spending money than everyone else in your crowd?
5. Cecily looked down on Hilary for copying Elgin's actions. Wasn't Cecily doing the same thing?
6. What are some verses from Scripture that tell you that stealing of any kind is wrong?

◆　◆　◆

Dear God, I'm ashamed to admit it, but sometimes I've been tempted to shoplift myself. It seems so easy just to grab something and run. The stores have so much, and I have so little money. Please help me to be honest, Lord.